1,2,3...
The
Toddler
Years

1,2,3...
The
Toddler
Years

A Practical Guide
for Parents and Caregivers

Irene Van der Zande

with

Santa Cruz Toddler Care Center Staff

Foreword by Magda Gerber

Santa Cruz
TODDLER CARE CENTER
Respect for Children

A publication of Toddler Center Press
Santa Cruz, California

1,2,3... The Toddler Years
A Practical Guide for Parents & Caregivers

Copyright © 2011 by Santa Cruz Toddler Care Center   Third Edition

Published by:

Santa Cruz
TODDLER CARE CENTER
1738 16th Avenue   *Respect for Children*
Santa Cruz, CA 95062

Printed in the United States of America

Dennis the Menace® cartoon "The Good Ol' Days" used by permission of Hank Ketcham and © by News America Syndicate

DISCLAIMER

The ideas in this book have all worked for the Santa Cruz Toddler Care Center. Children are individuals, however, and not all suggestions will be suitable for you and your child. The author and publisher advise you to use your common sense and your intimate knowledge of your own child. We cannot be held responsible for the misuse of any information in this book.

1. Toddlers – United States.   2. Child Raising – United States
3. Parenting – United States

ISBN 978-094095325-3
Library of Congress Catalog Card no.: 93-084405

Original designed by Ed Van der Zande. Cover photos by Nora Caruso and Raeleen Avila-Benabides. Cover by Tauna Coulson and Jesse Rose DeRooy. Text photos by Nora Caruso, Raeleen Avila-Benabides, Vickey LaMotte, Todd Tsukushi, and Brenna Henry. Photo on page 52 by Bill Lovejoy. Digital production and layout by Jesse Rose DeRooy.

To the toddlers, parents, board members and staff, who make the Santa Cruz Toddler Care Center the wonderful place it is. And to Infant Specialist MAGDA GERBER, whose philosophies and guidance provide the foundation for the Toddler Center Program.

Contents

Acknowledgments for the Third Edition

A S OF 2011, this book has been in print for 25 years. It is used as a textbook in Early Childhood Education classes throughout the country and as a parent resource throughout the world. For this edition we updated a number of the photos, while also leaving many of the legacy images. Together, they represent an interesting overview of 25 years of toddler care. As we carefully reviewed the text for this edition, we were struck with how appropriate this material continues to be despite all the parenting trends in the last few decades. This is echoed by the comments the Toddler Center receives from past families whose children are now grown. Respect for children builds respectful children, who become respectful adults.

This edition, like the Santa Cruz Toddler Care Center itself, reflects the vision and effort of many people. Sandy Davie, (right) Administrative Director at SCTCC, was Editor-in-Chief

with assistance from Program Director, Nora Bernheimer Caruso (right).

Nora Bernheimer Caruso also photographed, selected and edited the majority of the new pictures. Raeleen Avila-Benabides and Brenna Henry also contributed many photos to this edition.

Erin Barry took the picture in Chapter 22. Lisa Napier contributed the tantrum picture. Brian Lockwood took the picture in "Invaders From Inner Space".

Jennifer Vered, Nutritional Coordinator at SCTCC, created the recipes.

The cover was designed by Tauna Coulson. The front cover photo was taken by Raeleen Avila-Benabides. The back cover photos were taken by Nora Caruso and Raeleen Avila-Benabides.

Raphe Kudela did a technical review of the new pictures. Juniper Nichols helped format the photos and formatted part of the text.

Last, but in no way least, Jesse Rose DeRooy completed the digitalization process, compiling and reformatting the book in line with the original design while incorporating the new images. Her tireless effort was invaluable to the completion of this edition.

Acknowledgments
for the Original Edition

THIS BOOK IS the result of a four-year-long process involving the efforts of many people. All of their contributions are important. Most of all, though, credit must go to Toddler Center Co-Director Vickey LaMotte and to my husband, Ed Van der Zande. Their involvement was essential to the way this book reads and looks.

Vickey took responsibility by acting as editor of the book. She coordinated the review and publication process. She also provided many of the beautiful photographs.

Ed coordinated the typesetting and printing of the book, finding creative ways to keep quality high and costs low. He conceptually designed the layout. He also gave me tremendous personal support and encouragement.

The material from which this book was written

was gathered through extensive observations of and interviews with Toddler Center staff. Most of the interviews were provided by Vickey, her fellow Co-Director Lise Johnston, and former staff member Sharon Dowe. The countless hours they spent critiquing the materials, suggesting additional ideas and changes, added much to the scope of the book, and kept the Toddler Center philosophy clearly in focus.

The insights of a number of reviewers also added much to the scope and quality of the book. Reviewers were Ellen Bass, Eve Bertrandias, Anne and Bill Callahan, Mary Ann Dewey, Ellen Farmer, Judith Goodman, Rosemarie Greiner, Bruce Holgers, Tracy Johnson, Janis Keyser, Jenny Klein, Mary Larson; Candi Ledwich, Bill Leland, Maryanne Nolin, Helen Power, Raim, Lily, Ken and Elaine Regelson, Roberta Reyes, Karen Rossum, Diana Rothman, Judy Scarborough, Eric Schoeck, and Lucy Sloate.

For many years, the idea of a book had been discussed by many people familiar with the high quality of the Toddler Center program. In 1982, former Toddler Center Director Janet Gellman wrote a proposal to the Women's Foundation. Their funding made it possible for the Toddler Center to start working on the book.

Co-Director Lise Johnston held the project together in its early stages. She coordinated the work of Pamela King, Mary Larson, Tracye Lawson, and Noreen Winkler, who all contributed to the definition of what the book would cover and to the initial materials.

Lise also managed to find the only title everybody could live with.

Sharon Dowe contributed many of the thoughts in the "Successful Parenting" section. Her warmth and enthusiasm kept the project moving forward in its low moments.

Judith Goodman researched and organized the available literature. Eric Schoeck and Jenny Klein provided many of the ideas for the section on preventing child abuse. Betsy Isbister contributed greatly to the chapter on helping a child deal with grief. Anne Callahan typed the rough drafts. Eve Bertrandias' research assistance greatly furthered the marketing effort.

In addition to Vickey's pictures, several photographs were taken by Todd Tsukushi of Santa Cruz Photographics. The photo in the chapter on "Saying Good-bye is Sad" was taken by Bill Lovejoy of the Santa Cruz Sentinel.

Over the years, the project grew greatly in scope from the small booklet originally envisioned to a full-sized book. The Greater Santa Cruz County Community Foundation came to the rescue with a timely grant to help with the first printing, which brought the project to a successful completion.

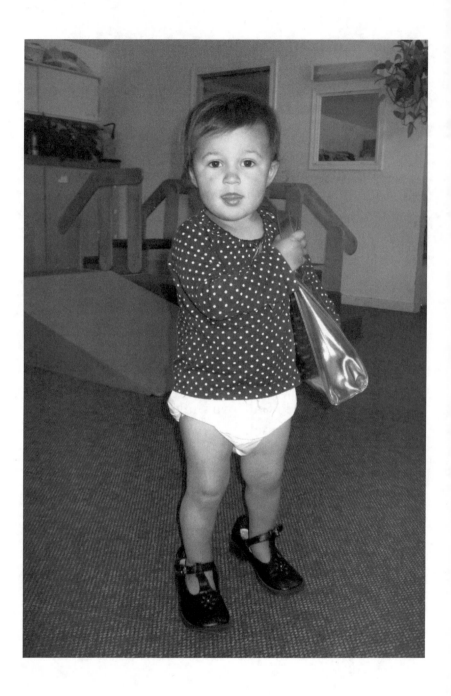

Foreword
by
Magda Gerber

WHEN I WAS asked to review the first draft of *1, 2, 3...The Toddler Years*, I thought "Oh no. Not another manuscript to read!" But I have always loved the Santa Cruz Toddler Care Center, so I ignored the big stack of written material waiting for me and started 1, 2, 3... and I couldn't stop. It was a pure joy to read something so clearly and simply written.

This book is a description of how the Toddler Center cares for young children. Through many true-life examples, the book demonstrates the philosophy and practice of respect for young children which is advocated by Resources for Infant Educarers (RIE) founded by Dr. Tom Forrest and myself.

To read such a book made me proud because of my long association with the Santa Cruz Toddler Center. It all started when, in their search for a model to use for their new center, co-founders Catherine Boxer and Kate Kelly with her husband Jim, visited the Demonstration Infant Program which was a predecessor of RIE. Their reaction was enthusiastic: "We saw so many places, and we were becoming increasingly discouraged. Finally, we know how we want to run our toddler program!"

Soon after the Toddler Center opened, Kate and Catherine invited me to come and give them feedback. I was pleased to see that they really had understood the essence of our philosophy and were able to put a great deal of it into practice in a child care setting. When Kate and Catherine left the Center, I thought sadly, "As the Directors go, the vision will be lost." Since then, although many changes have happened, new directors, new staff, and a new location, the original spirit has survived. Each time I return to the Toddler Center, I find that the RIE philosophy of respect is still alive and well.

Why is this so unusual? After my talks and seminars around the country, people from the audience usually tell me. "Oh, that's exactly how we treat our babies." However, when I visit these programs I don't find that to be the case. It is easy to agree with our theory. Few people would admit that they don't respect children. To practice respect in each interaction with the child, however, is more difficult than just understanding the theory.

Another thing people often tell me is "It sounds so wonderful, but it wouldn't work in *our* situation. There is so much pressure. Each parent wants something different. We have such high staff turnover. So many children are coming and going." I agree it isn't easy, but, as we learn from this book, it *can* be done.

A program which is guided by the RIE philosophy must develop an approach which is understood by all parents and staff, including substitutes. This book goes a long way toward explaining how the RIE philosophy works on a day-to-day basis. With this understanding, the happy environment and calm atmosphere of a RIE program will attract those parents who would value and support it. Staff members who learn to practice the RIE philosophy will find meaning and enjoyment rather than burnout in their jobs, because under the right conditions, toddlers are enjoyable and fascinating people.

It makes me sad that I cannot share this book with Dr. Emmi Pikler who died in 1984. She was the person who originated this whole approach to young children. She would have appreciated the way her philosophy is brought to life in the United States where so many trends influence people who work in the field of infant/toddler care.

Dr. Pikler was a pediatrician in Hungary who first taught her philosophy to the parents of her patients. In 1946, she implemented her approach in a residential setting: the "Loczy" Institute in Budapest. The original name of the Institute was the National Methodological Institute for Residential Nurseries. In 1985, it was renamed the Emmi Pikler National Methodological Institute for Residential Nurseries in her honor. The goal of the Institute is to provide an environment in which young children can reach their full potential, despite being brought up in an institution. Research done on Pikler children in their later years shows that, unlike children raised in most institutions, they grow up into healthy, capable individuals who are able to make a good adjustment to family life.

Reading this book is like looking through a one-way mirror into daily life with a toddler. The many lively examples carry the philosophy, and both the toddlers' and their carers' point of view is emphasized. We learn the "why" of toddlers' actions and how we can respond with respect in all our interactions with them.

Although the teachers are called caregivers in this book, I would like to honor them with my own term "educarers" because they educate the children through the loving, respectful way that they care for them.

I would like all my students to have the chance to visit the Santa Cruz Toddler Care Center. The closest thing to experiencing the Center in reality is reading and absorbing **1,2,3...The Toddler Years**. I hope all of your readers – parents, family day care providers, infant/toddler caregivers, students, and people interested in young children – will enjoy this book as much as I did.

Magda Gerber

Magda Gerber

Introduction

A S PARENTS OF toddlers, we lead full and busy
lives. It's easy to get caught up in the moment.
Yet once in a while, we all find ourselves asking. "What
kind of a life do we really want for our children? How
do we want them to feel about themselves? How does
what we do affect their growth and well-being?"

Questions like these help us look beyond the
moment and make decisions on how we're going
to handle the many issues we face as parents and
caregivers.

The Santa Cruz Toddler Care Center was
founded in 1976 by two women who were concerned
about the lack of quality care for young children.
The experience of decades of work with thousands
of children has confirmed the belief that what
young children learn about themselves and their
world during their toddler years will affect the rest

of their lives. The Center's philosophy focuses on the development and communication of genuine respect for each toddler. This philosophy guides the practical ways the caregivers work with the children day by day.

The Santa Cruz Toddler Care Center has grown into a model program visited by people from all over. The Toddler Center provides quality care to young children and offers support and education to their parents. Full- and part-time schedules make it possible for parents to work or go to school. Funding provided by the City and County of Santa Cruz enables the Center to keep costs affordable for low- and middle-income families. It's a special kind of place. Happy . . . peaceful . . . busy . . . calm . . . safe . . . loving.

As described in the Foreword, the Toddler Center uses the approach presented by Infant Care Specialist Magda Gerber. Although based on the philosophy evolving from Magda Gerber's approach, this is a "how-to" book, not one on theory. The goal of this book is to help parents at home, as well as caregivers in centers, make the most of the toddler years. The examples used are based on real-life experiences at the Toddler Center and in children's homes.

Parenting a toddler is a difficult job. This book describes ways of respecting our children's needs while still addressing our own needs. Trying out the methods described here can, in the long run, make parenting toddlers easier and more fun. At the same time, these ideas can help promote our toddlers' growth and self-confidence.

In today's society, many different people may take on the role of parent to a toddler besides the child's biological mother and father. A toddler may be "parented" by one parent, grandparents, foster parents, stepparents, two mothers, or two fathers. The word "parents" in this book refers to anyone who has long-term, on-going responsibility for a child's well-being and care.

Due to the work of Magda Gerber and others, there are a large number of excellent childcare centers and individual caregivers basing their approach on a similar philosophy. It is hoped that this book will lead to even greater understanding and more widespread use of this philosophy of care.

Part One

Respect for Toddlers.
What Does This Mean
and How Can We
Make It Work?

THE TODDLER AGE. It starts somewhere around a child's first birthday and continues until about the age of three. This is a time of amazing growth for children and challenge for their parents. In just two short years, young children go from crawling to running and climbing. The few words they can say quickly turn into full sentences and soon into long discussions about big ideas.

Toddlers have the right to be accepted and respected for who they are *now*. Not dependent babies. But also not yet capable preschoolers. Respect means:

- treating each child as a special individual with important thoughts, feelings, and needs.
- giving children the opportunity to grow and learn at their own pace.

- allowing children the freedom to create and master their own challenges.

This is an age when children are constantly on the move. They learn about the world by exploring it. They want to do everything right now all by themselves. This can be frustrating both for the children and their parents. Toddlers so often want to do more than they can, or than we'll let them. This is why the toddler age is sometimes referred to as the "terrible two's."

The methods described in the following chapters show how to meet the challenges of the toddler age in ways that respect the needs of the children - and of the people who live with them. "At first I was doubtful," says the father of two-year-old Evan. "This is sure different from the way I was brought up. But I kept seeing how well Evan did at the Center. It took a while for me to get used to doing things this way, but it's worth it. I enjoy Evan a lot more now. I used to waste so much time being mad at the things he'd say or do. Now I can accept his need to try out these things as part of his growing independence. And I can stop him in a way I feel good about when his actions go against his staying safe or affect other people's rights, including my own."

1

Let Me Choose

"LET'S PLAY SCHOOL, CHAD. I'll be the teacher, you be the kid." Jenny handed her 18-month-old brother some paper and a crayon, and added, "You can draw a picture and I'll write your name on it."

Chad cuddled next to his five-year-old sister. "Mama!" Jenny yelled. "Guess what Chad needs!"

Their mother came right over. "Let's change your diaper, Chad."

Chad looked away from his mother. "No."

"Chad. I see you're really enjoying playing school with Jenny. You can play a few more minutes while I get ready."

Their mother laid out the diapers, ointment, and washcloth. Then she came up to Chad again. "Chad. You've really worked hard on that picture. Now, let's go change that diaper."

"No," Chad growled.

"I need to change your diaper. Do you want to bring your picture with you or leave it here?"

Chad grabbed his paper. "Do you want to walk by yourself or be carried?" Chad lifted his arms to be carried.

Jenny laughed, "I bet he'll be glad when he's big like me and doesn't have everybody bossing him around!"

Toddlers may not be able to say many words, but they can sure let us know how they feel about all those people who keep telling them what to do. "No!" "Not now!" "Go away!"

Just like all of us, toddlers are happier when they have some control over their lives. Chad's mother could have ignored what he said. It might have been faster for her just to pick him up and get him cleaned up right away. Of course, if he got mad and started wiggling, it might have been a harder job. By waiting, Chad's mother showed respect for his interest in what he was doing with his sister. By offering him choices (take the picture or leave it; walk or be carried), she gave him a chance to say something about what was happening to him. She let Chad know that his thoughts and actions were important to her and let him feel a part of what was going on. This made it easier for him to accept what he didn't have a choice about.

Of course, it's important to set limits. At the same time, offering choices wherever possible within these limits gives even very young children the feeling that they have control.

There's almost always a way to give our toddlers a choice, with a little preparation and imagination, it becomes possible to ask, "Do you want to:

- do it now or wait a few minutes?
- eat cereal or eggs?
- have a blue cup or an orange one?
- drink water or juice?
- stop hitting Maria by yourself, or have me help you?
- come over here by yourself or have me come get you?"

Notice that these choices are all offered in the form of closed questions like, "Do you want to wear your red pants or your blue pants?" It's important before asking the question to decide what choices we're willing to live with. Open questions such as "What do you want to wear?" lead to answers we may not be willing to accept like, "Nothing!" One mother found that she had to watch out for the question "What do you want for breakfast?" because her kids would always pick blueberry pancakes!

The choices offered must be real ones for the child. When there is no choice, we need to be careful not to offer one by mistake. In our grown-up world, orders are often worded as questions for politeness. When our boss asks, "Could you step into my office for a moment?" most of us know we'd better say, "Yes," unless there's an awfully good reason.

To toddlers, these polite "fake" questions can be confusing and upsetting. If we ask a happily playing toddler, "Are you ready to take your nap now?" she's sure to yell, "No!" If we're not sure a child will cooperate, we sometimes soften our statements by adding, "Okay?" as in "I'm going to leave now. Okay?" By making this a question, we give the child a choice we really didn't mean to offer. It's possible to say something clearly and still give a choice; for example, "It's time for you to take your nap now. Do you want to bring the book with you or leave it here?"

Just like adults, young children may need a

moment to make up their minds. It's important, when offering a choice, to give a child a chance to think. If the child has trouble making the decision, we can repeat the choices. "Do you want to wear your sweater or your jacket?" If the child can't decide after a reasonable period of time, it's time to take charge: "I'll help you choose so we can leave. Here's your jacket."

Being able to make decisions is an important skill at any age. Giving our children chances to have real choices about what they do and what happens to them helps them to grow in self-esteem and confidence.

2

My Feelings Should Be Free

"YOU KNOW I never let you have candy, so quit yelling!"

"Why are you whining? You never played with that toy anyway."

"Stop crying! You aren't really hurt."

Words like these usually lead to more yelling, more whining, and more tears. Young children can have very strong feelings about things that may seem silly to grown-ups. But mad, scared, unhappy feelings don't go away just because someone says they're wrong. It's much better for our toddlers if we respect their right to have these feelings.

A good example is the approach used by Roy one morning when two-year-old Jill wouldn't get into her car seat.

"No!" she said, pointing to the driver's seat. "I

sit dere!"

"I know you had fun sitting there yesterday, Jill," Roy explained, "But that was when the car was parked. Today, I need to drive you to childcare and me to work. And I need you to get into your car seat."

"No! No car seat!" yelled Jill, "I drive."

"I know you're mad, Jill. Look, here's your little car. Suppose you drive your car while I drive my car."

"No!" sobbed Jill.

"It's getting late," sighed Roy. "Jill. I know you wish you could drive the big car. I want you in the car seat so you'll be safe. Do you want to climb in yourself or do you need me to help you?"

Jill kept yelling and began hitting with her arms and legs. Roy picked her up and put her into the car seat, talking to her in a calm voice. "Jill, it looks like you need help even though it makes you mad. I know you don't want to be in that car seat, but I'm still going to buckle you in. Here's your little car if you want it. Phew! Let's go. Bye, house."

"Bye house!" echoed Jill, smiling through her tears and waving, the toy car clutched in her hand.

Jill's upset feelings must have seemed way beyond reason to Roy. But he let her see that it was okay to have these feelings. As an adult, he was able to put aside his own annoyed feelings when she acted that way. We can hope that Roy found someone to tell later that day, "Would you believe what Jill did this morning!"

At the Toddler Center, caregivers spend a lot of time giving children names for their feelings.

"You put that puzzle together all by yourself. You look proud."

"You're crying because you're missing your mommy. You sound sad."

"You're yelling because Joey took that truck away from you. You seem angry."

"Yes, we're going to have lunch right now. You look happy."

Caregivers talk about all kinds of feelings but do not label some feelings as "good" and others as "bad." If they did, the children might try to hide their unhappy "bad" feelings. It's much healthier for children, and adults, to be open with these feelings instead of pushing them away.

When children are upset, they have a hard time listening to someone else. When Jerald cried because his balloon had popped, his big brother said, "Well, baby, what do you expect when you poke a balloon with a stick?" Of course, Jerald just cried harder.

His mother came close to him and said. "You're really sad that your balloon popped. That loud bang was scary too. You had so much fun playing with that big red balloon and now it's gone." Jerald calmed down and looked up at his mother, who then said gently. "Balloons do break when you poke them with sticks. That's just how balloons are."

When toddlers are unhappy, we may be tempted to get them to think about something else. They're so little, and we want them to feel better fast. If a child falls, it's hard not to swoop down, pick the child up, and say, "Oh, ouch! Don't cry! Look. I'll read you a book!" Changing the subject like this can give toddlers the idea that there's something wrong with feeling upset. Instead, we can better help children by talking about their feelings and offering comfort when it's needed.

When Kimiko cried at the Toddler Center, her caregiver, Joan, moved up close and said, "Kimiko,

I hear you crying really hard. You didn't like Becky knocking over your trains. That made you mad." Joan sat near Kimiko and kept talking about what had happened. Then she asked, "Do you want to sit in my lap?" Kimiko waited a minute, then crawled in. Joan cuddled her and said, "You were really upset. I'm glad you're feeling better now."

If Kimiko had stayed upset and not been ready to accept comfort, Joan would have stayed close and kept talking with her about what was happening. She would have said, "You're still upset. I'm here to help you if you need me." If Kimiko had continued to cry, Joan might have then said, "It looks like you need to cry a little longer. That's okay. I'll stay with you until you feel better. If you want a hug, come over here."

Children need to understand their feelings. They need to know that their uncomfortable feelings are just as important as their pleasant feelings. By accepting these feelings, we teach our toddlers to accept themselves and each other.

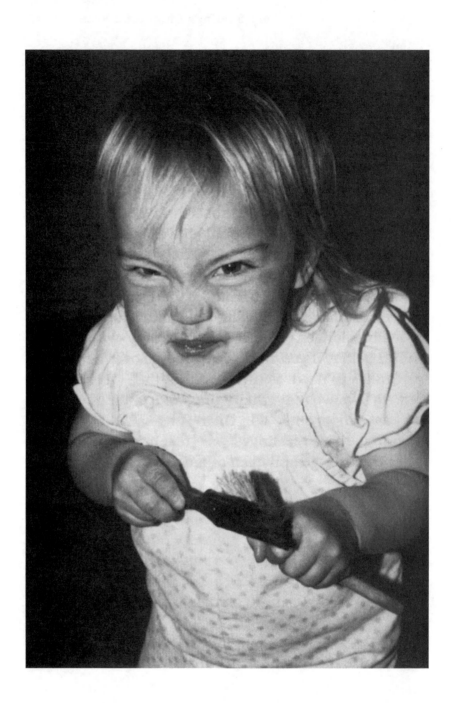

3

Stop Me When Enough's Enough

"*HOW INTERESTING.*" *JoJo seems to think, "Mommy gets mad if I spit on the table! . . . Was that just at breakfast or also at lunch? . . . What about dinner? . . . Just yesterday, or also today? . . . It seems okay to spit in the bathtub . . . She made me spit out a bug . . . what if I spit on these papers on her desk?*"

Parents of two-year-olds may be forgiven for sometimes wondering if their children are really going to drive them crazy. All too often, we see our young children give us "the toddler look," that quick, impish glance that says, "I'm going to do something you won't like. What are you gonna do about it?" It's not that our toddlers are really out to get us. Just as babies need to learn where their bodies stop and the world begins, toddlers need to figure out what happens when they do things. The way they learn is by trying out all kinds of behavior and finding out what comes next.

The children of some lucky parents seem to learn their limits overnight. Other children need to test us with certain behaviors over and over for weeks or even months. It helps to keep in mind that this is normal. Just because our toddlers keep hitting, kicking, grabbing, biting, tearing, breaking, climbing, or throwing, doesn't mean that they are going to be doing this for the rest of their lives. After listening to many complaints, Phil's grandmother told her son, "Phil's a little angel compared to what you were like at his age. You grew out of it. So will he."

What toddlers need from us are clear, consistent messages telling them when to stop. A calm, matter-of-fact tone of voice works better than an angry one. Limits can be stated in firm but respectful words. We can do this by using what is called an "I" message. That is, instead of saying "You must do this," we can make it clear that we are speaking for ourselves.

"I want you to be gentle."

"I need you to help me get your clothes on."

"I don't like it when you run away."

We can talk about what the child is doing rather than using blaming or labeling words like "You're bad." When possible, we can also give the child a reason and a safe way to try out the behavior. When necessary, we can say what will happen next if the child doesn't do what we want. And we can accept our child's unhappy feelings about being stopped.

"I want you to put that toy down. It belongs here. It will be here when you come back, but I want you to let go of it now ... You're still holding on tight. If you can't let go by yourself, I'll help you open your fingers."

"I don't like it when you wave your shovel so close to Demarr's face. You might hurt him... You didn't move it away by yourself, so I had to stop your hand."

"I don't like it when you tear the pages out of that book, Kati. That ruins the book and we can't enjoy it. I hear you crying and I know you still want the book. I'll have to put this book away until we fix it. Here are some old newspapers you can tear up."

It can be hard to keep telling our toddlers the same things over and over. As one mother said, "I don't know a parent who hasn't given in once in awhile. Our kids know just when our defenses are down and seem to test us most when we're tired or busy or embarrassed."

So sometimes we blow it. At the end of a long day we might let our child play with the toothpaste, just to buy ourselves a few extra minutes to sit quietly and read the newspaper. The best way out the next time the child wants the toothpaste is to be honest about what happened, but still be firm. "I was tired yesterday, and I didn't stop you from squeezing out the toothpaste.

But, now..."

Although caregivers often need to physically stop a child's actions at the Toddler Center, they never hit children. Spanking may send the message that it really is okay to hurt someone else. To teach gentle behavior, we need to show it.

Toddlers test limits to find out about themselves and other people. By stopping children in a firm but respectful way when they push our limits, we're helping them to figure out their world and to feel safe.

Giving Anger a Safe Place to Go

When her mother left the Toddler Center, Vanessa cried at the door. She wouldn't let anyone comfort her. After a few minutes, she walked up to a smaller child and pushed him. The caregiver, Susan, moved close

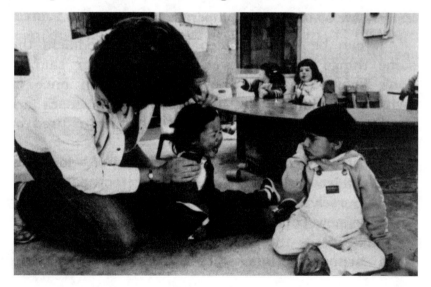

to Vanessa and said "Vanessa, you pushed Jake. You seem really mad." Then Vanessa tried to hit another child. Susan quickly and gently stopped her and moved her body in front of Vanessa. "Vanessa, I'm not going to let you hit kids."

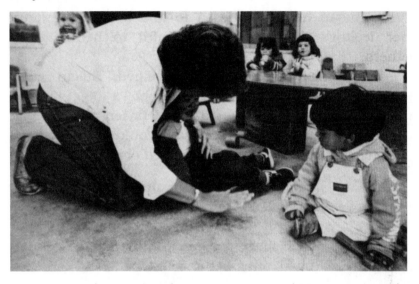

Gently putting her arms around Vanessa so she wouldn't run away, Susan kept talking to her with a caring voice. "You look mad. Seems like you're angry about your mom leaving. She'll come back after your nap. Even if you're mad, Vanessa, I'm not going to let you hurt your friends. You can hit those balls with a soft bat." Vanessa angrily swatted at a hanging ball with the bat. When she was finished, she gave a big sigh. She gave Susan a smile, then ran off to play.

Young children often show their angry feelings by hurting other kids. Vanessa was feeling mad at her mother, and she let her anger out by pushing. It was important for Susan to stop Vanessa so other children wouldn't be scared or hurt. At the same time, Susan looked for the reason behind Vanessa's actions. She let Vanessa know that her anger toward her mother was okay. In suggesting that she play with the soft bats, Susan helped Vanessa to find a way to express her feelings that was not harmful to herself or to others.

If using the soft bats hadn't helped, Susan might have suggested that Vanessa kick a ball or push a bike. If Vanessa had chosen to stay mad instead of accepting help, Susan would have let her - as long as Vanessa didn't hurt herself or other kids.

4

I Can Understand More
Than You Think

"OH, HELLO CUTIE PIE!" said the elderly lady in the park, "Can you talk yet, little fellow?" Two-year-old Brian stopped pouring sand into his pocket. His mouth fell open and he looked up at the lady, "What's the matter? Cat got your tongue?" she laughed. "Now tell me your name, cutie. Come on, what's your name?"

Brian looked away from the lady, comforted by the sight of his mother and older sister close by, "Well," the lady said, annoyed by his silence, "I guess you can't understand me; you're still a baby, Goo Goo! Bye Bye!" She patted Brian on the head and walked away.

Brian's big sister climbed to the top of the slide and yelled after the lady. "He can so understand! He can even talk! He just didn't want to talk to you!"

When young children are learning to talk, they may not be able to answer our questions. That doesn't mean they don't understand when *we* talk with *them.* The lady in the park put Brian on the spot by trying to make him tell his name. She might have made friends if, instead, she had started by just talking about what Brian was doing, "Oh, I see you're having a good time with that sand."

Until our toddlers start to use a lot of words, it's easy to forget to talk with them. But at this age, they are learning to speak with amazing speed. In just two short years, they'll grow from one-year-olds, who can only say a few or no words, to three-year-olds, who talk our ears off!

Long before they can say a lot themselves, even very young toddlers can understand us if we speak in simple, short sentences. We can talk to our toddlers about:

- what has happened: "Yes, this morning I spilled the cat food and it made a mess. You helped clean it up."
- what is happening: "You're touching your bellybutton. Yes, Timmy has a bellybutton, too. So do I."
- and what is going to happen next: "I'll watch you stack up those blocks . . . Yes, when you push them over they'll go boom! . . . Then it will be time for me to help you get ready for

your nap." (This is a good way to help our toddlers get ready for change without being taken by surprise.)

Our goal is to help children learn to communicate. Even children who can't talk yet can let us know what they want and need. By paying attention to their sounds, gestures, and facial expressions, we let them know that we take their feelings seriously even before they have many words at their command. When children do begin to use more words, they have more power. If Leslie can say, "I want that!" she may not need to grab. If Roy yells, "I'm mad at you!" he might not need to hit. And Ben, who likes to tell people "I love you," is given lots of love.

It's important to show respect to a child who is learning to speak. Sometimes it's hard not to laugh at the funny ways children put their words together. Many people think this is cute and copy the child by speaking in a shrill voice and using baby talk. Most of us find ourselves doing this occasionally. However, toddlers will learn more if, instead of using baby talk, we speak in a normal voice using short sentences and simple words. If we correct our toddlers when they say words "wrong," it just discourages them. Instead, we can use "their" words along with the right ones. "Yes, Betsy, you can have your blankie now. It's a nice soft blanket, isn't it?"

Sometimes children surprise us by using language we don't like. The first time, they're just copying words they've heard from others. Soon they find out the attention getting value of these particular words and use them over and over - usually at moments when the person most likely to be offended is present. It can be hard, but since children are using these words to get a reaction, the best way to get them to stop is to pay no attention at all.

As parents, we often worry about the speed with which our toddlers learn to speak. One mother laughed, "I used to think about it all the time. I compared Jeri to other two-year-olds who seemed to know so many words. I kept thinking, 'If only she could talk!' Now she's a teenager, and when she's on the phone with her friend, I find myself thinking, 'If only she'd stop talking!' "

Toddlers will learn to talk in their own way at their own time. Our job is to help by giving them many chances to hear and use speech.

5

Let Me Work It Out For Myself

KIDS FIGURE OUT what they want to do and how they want to do it all the time. We adults are far too quick to jump in before they have the chance. It's often tempting for us to just take over. But toddlers learn much more by finding out how to do things for themselves than by having everything done for them.

When a child needs help at the Toddler Center, there are three things that always happen:

- a caregiver comes up close to the child and pays attention.
- the caregiver waits to see what the child can do for herself or himself.
- the caregiver gives just enough help so that the child can succeed.

When Corey's tricycle tipped over, he lay with his foot stuck under the wheel, wailing loudly. His caregiver, Jeff, walked over quickly and knelt next to him. Instead of picking Corey up, Jeff said calmly, "Uh oh! Your bike fell. Now your foot is stuck." Corey stopped crying, but still lay on the ground, whining.

Jeff waited a moment, then said, "If you want to get up, you could use your hand to push the wheel off your foot." They waited another few moments together, then Corey wriggled free and hopped cheerfully back onto the tricycle.

By being close, Jeff was able to see that Corey was not hurt and to let Corey know that he was not alone. Jeff gave Corey time to find his own way out. Instead of taking over by picking Corey up and putting him on his feet, Jeff offered him one suggestion. If Corey had stayed stuck, Jeff would then have helped him push off the wheel.

Parents visiting the Toddler Center are often amazed by how many different things toddlers can do for themselves. Many toddlers can...

- bring a chair to the snack table.
- open their cubbies, put their things in and close the doors.
- put on their shoes as well as take them off.
- put on their own clothes.
- feed themselves.

Toddlers like to feel independent. They learn quickly if we start with what they can do and help them do more in small steps. "If you want to go outside, Lucy, you need to put on your jacket. Can you bring it here? . . . It's by the wall over there . . . You got it! Now can you put it on? . . . Stick your hand in this hole right here. Stick it all the way through . . . that's great! Now, this hand goes through the other hole . . . I'll get the zipper started. Now pull up this little tab here . . . Look at that! You put on your jacket!" Of course, doing this takes more time than just putting Lucy's jacket on for her. But pretty soon, she'll be doing it all by herself.

Encouraging our toddlers to do what they can for themselves not only helps to build their self confidence, but also means that we as parents won't need to do

so much for them in the long run. Children who are confident in their ability to learn through practice are more likely to grow into independent people, who will be able to take charge of their lives, making things happen rather than waiting for things to happen to them.

6

I Need Special Time
With <u>You</u>

AFTER A LONG day at the office, Marcie came home to a mess. Dirty dishes were stacked so high, she didn't even have room to get dinner started. "Why didn't I do these this morning?" she groaned.

Just then, two-and-a-half year-old Eric ran into the room shouting. "Play with me, Mommy!"

"I can't. Too many dishes. Anyway, you played all day with Betsy. She even took you to the zoo. Remember?" Marcie found the plug for the sink, squirted in some soap, and turned on the water.

Eric paused as if thinking, "How can I make Mommy understand?" Then he tugged at Marcie's pants and said. "Play, Mommy! Play! PLAY!"

"I spent so much time with him yesterday." Marcie sighed to herself. "Can't he take care of himself and leave me alone for even a minute?" She glared down into the wistful face of her little boy. "Why does he always want to be with me?" Suddenly

31

her grumpiness was gone. "I'm so glad that he does want to be with me!"

With soapy hands, she pulled a chair up to the sink. "Climb up here. We'll play washing dishes and talking together."

Eric's face lit up with a huge smile. "Okay!"

The dishes got clean. Soapy water splashed onto the floor. "It was dirty anyway," said Marcie. "What animals did you see at the zoo?"

Children need attention from the people they love. It's not enough just to take care of the physical needs like keeping our toddlers fed, dressed, and clean. It's important for our children to feel that we *like* to spend time with them.

Most toddlers will not be as clear about their

needs as Eric was. They might give signs which are not so pleasant, like being whiney and willful. Like spilling the milk on purpose. Or asking over and over for something they know they can't have. As a pediatrician pointed out, "It's human to be angry when our kids get like this. It might help to look at it from their point of view. Try asking yourself, 'How long has it been since my child has had me all to her or himself?' "

Toddlers live in the here and now. Yesterday is ancient history, and tomorrow might just as well be next year. So, for a toddler, many little special moments every day count more than big events now and then. What makes the time special for our toddlers is not what the activity is. It's having the undivided attention of the most important people in their world: us!

At an evening workshop about quality time, parents easily came up with a bunch of ideas for making routine activities special:

- "When we're going someplace in the car, I take a word Leslie says and make a silly song out of it."

- "Jerry sits in the bath with his own sponge and helps me scrub the tub."

- "I take 15 minutes each evening to watch, really sit and watch and do nothing else, while Sarah plays in her room. I talk with her about what she's doing and how she's doing it. She calls it our 'alone-together' time and looks forward to it a lot."

The real problem, the parents agreed, was that they needed time for themselves so much that it was hard to make these special moments happen very often for their toddlers. What if, in the first example, Marcie had been really upset and needed to sort things out? She might not have been able to make a game out of washing the dishes. She would then have needed to say something to Eric like, "I need time alone right now. I'll play with you after dinner. Do you want to listen to music or to look at these books?"

Some parents felt that the special times together never seemed to happen. One father in the group said, "Sometimes, after Mel is asleep, I feel I want to wake her up and start the day over. We've been so busy that I haven't spent a moment really being *with* her at all. It takes so much time just to keep up with what has to be done - like changing diapers, making meals, and cleaning up messes. How can I spend quality time with her?"

At the Toddler Center, routine caregiving times, like diapering, are seen as opportunities to give each child special attention from one adult. As much as possible, the child is helped to be part of what's going on. There's lots of talk. Most of the words may come from the caregiver, but by waiting for the child's response, the caregiver makes sure that the communication goes both ways. "It's time for your diaper change, Susie . . . Do you want to walk or shall I carry you? . . . Here we are at the changing table . . .

Do you want to climb up yourself or shall I lift you?. . . Your pants are all wet, aren't they? . . . Can you help me pull them off? . . . Thanks . . . Yes, I see your tummy. . . Here is a warm washcloth to wipe the pee off your bottom. Do you want to touch the cloth? . . . Yes, it feels *soft* . . . Time to put your diaper on . . . can you lift your bottom? . . . Can you help me put your pants on? . . . Now, do you want to climb down yourself or do you want me to carry you?"

To someone watching, it's amazing! How can the caregivers say and do the same things over and over

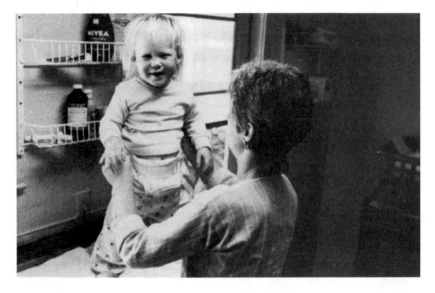

day after day and still sound cheerful and interested each time with each child? One caregiver explains, "Diapering time gives me the chance to slow down and enjoy one child. I learn about each child's unique way of doing things. It's exciting to see how much children learn just from changing diapers in this way. They find out how to cooperate with an adult, help with their own care, and communicate their wants and needs. Instead of being just a chore, diapering becomes a joyful time for both of us."

7

Plan Ahead . . . It Helps

"TODAY WAS AWFUL!" groaned Dan to his wife after a long day with Kathy, their 14-month old daughter. I didn't get a thing done. I tried to do the laundry, but Kathy poured all the soap on the floor. As soon as we got that cleaned up, your folks called. Kathy wouldn't say a word on the phone. Then she began climbing up my leg and whining because she was hungry. There wasn't a thing in the house she wanted to eat, so we went shopping. Kathy screamed the whole time we were in the store because I wouldn't let her eat a banana before we bought it. Then she almost ran in front of a car in the parking lot. I had to drop the groceries to catch her. I thought a visit to the park would do us both good, but she was so tired that she kept crying and throwing sand at the other kids. Thank goodness she fell asleep in the car on the way back. I'm really glad you're home. I am going to bed!"

The best way to avoid a day like Dan's is to plan ahead. Dan was doing what he usually did, but now Kathy was no longer the cuddly baby who, awake or asleep, cheerfully went along for the ride. She'd become an active, independent toddler, trying to take charge of her world.

Young children have a lot of energy. Their curiosity and drive to explore can make things hard for us as parents and caregivers. From our point of view, they get into everything! Yet, this exploration is a normal and healthy way for them to learn about the world around them.

An area that is both safe and exciting can let a toddler put this drive to explore to good use. High quality toddler programs offer an ideal way to do this. The Toddler Center, for instance, has been set up and organized with the needs and wants of toddlers in mind. The physical space, the equipment, and the variety of toys all help to build a toddler's sense of independence and to reduce the need for adult direction. Shelves are at the children's level. The equipment is designed for toddlers. Indoor and outdoor areas are as free as possible from dangerous items. Caregivers are always close by to watch and to help children as needed. Toddlers know what to expect during the day - when they'll play, eat and sleep.

"It's amazing, *everything* is planned," said one mother after watching for a day. "There are even extra boxes of tissues all over the place so no one will have to walk too far to get a clean tissue for tears or a runny nose."

At the Toddler Center, the reason adults are there is to take care of the children. As parents, we have other work and other family members to worry about. That makes the job harder. There are bound to be times when our toddlers' needs and our own are very different.

Toddler: Take me out!
Parent: I've got to get this done.

Toddler: Watch me!
Parent: I want to read right now.

Toddler: What's that?

Parent: Don't touch that; it's the ____!

Of course, we can't always structure our plans around our toddlers; this wouldn't be healthy for us or our children. Sometimes, we have to cramp our toddler's style in order to get things done. It wouldn't be good for our toddlers or our family if we ordered our lives around this one small person. But we want to be sure there are other times when we do plan around our toddlers needs, and let our own needs wait. It's amazing how a little planning ahead can make a world of difference in the quality of time we have with our children.

After his hard day with 14-month-old Kathy, Dan promised himself that their next full day alone together would be better. The evening before, Dan made sure there were enough clean clothes and food. He thought about what he wanted to do, both for Kathy and himself: "take a walk together . . . read the newspaper . . . buy groceries . . . fix the drain . . . well, maybe the drain better wait . . . and maybe I'd better fix Kathy a snack before we go to the store."

The next morning, Dan and Kathy had a great breakfast together. They talked about the food ("yum!"), the rain ("wet!"), and their plan ("go out!"). Just as they were ready to go out the door in rubber boots and raincoats, the telephone rang. Thinking there might be some emergency, Dan answered the phone. It was his parents, wanting to chat. "We're just leaving," Dan said firmly, glancing at the impatient little figure by the door. "I'll call you back this afternoon when Kathy is napping." Then he and Kathy splashed happily off into the rain.

Plans work best when they take into account each child's needs, abilities, and interests. If two-year-old Juan hates car trips, but loves to look at books, a large box of books will make a long ride more pleasant. If three-year-old Sandy can't sit still until she's run off some energy, it might be a good idea to visit the park before the library. Of course, just to make our lives interesting, our toddlers don't stay the same month by month, week by week, or even day by day. As one father put it, "Never get used to anything. Once you think you've got your kids figured out, they change!"

Another part of planning that's easy to forget is how important it is to keep our promises. Think how we feel when someone breaks an appointment with us with no warning and no reason. Young children feel the same way. They get upset when we say we'll read a book right away and then run to answer the phone. How often does our "I'll be done in just a minute" turn into a pretty long time? "I guess Gen got tired of waiting for us to stop talking," groaned Yoko to her neighbor as she started to clean up the mess made by her two-year-old son. "But did he have to dump out the whole box of cereal? Oh, well, if I'd kept my promise to him to go out on our walk right away, this wouldn't have happened."

Sometimes, a change of plans can't be helped. When this happens, we can help our toddlers accept the situation by explaining what's going on. "I know you're upset. I said we'd go to the park and now I'm changing the tire. But the car won't run with a flat tire. Once the tire is fixed, we'll go. How about helping me?"

Sometimes we'll have a hard day with our toddlers no matter what we do, but planning ahead gives us a better chance of having things go well.

Keep In Mind That . . .

Planning for Environment means arranging safe places indoors and outdoors where a toddler can play with as few "no's" as possible.

Planning for Schedules means setting up regular times for naps, meals, and active play, and preparing the child for change between one type of activity and another. The child's high and low energy times of the day should be kept in mind.

Planning for Activities means arranging times when the child can explore lots of materials, play structures, open areas, and people. This could be at a park, play group, or child care program as well as at home.

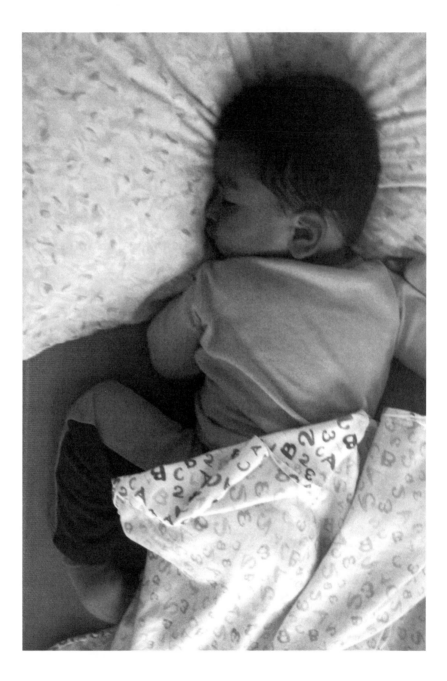

8

I'm Not Sleepy

WHEN YOU LOOK at this peacefully sleeping child, you'd never know how much struggle it took to get him to go to bed.

On the subject of sleep, there are no easy answers. Even the experts seem to have opposite points of view. Some say our children may need to cry to be able to relax enough to go to sleep. Others say that children who are left alone crying may feel frightened and unloved.

And while the experts are arguing, our toddlers are often not getting to sleep, and we're getting worn out. As one-year-old Oriana's mother said, "At bedtime I'm so tired and Oriana's so crabby, I get *really* frustrated. Night after night I try everything. Why won't she just go to sleep?"

We can't *make* our toddlers go to sleep, but we can find ways to help them put themselves to sleep. We can talk about sleeping. What being tired looks and feels like. "Your eyes are droopy. You keep bumping into things." And how we feel and what we do when our own bodies are tired. "That big yawn was my body telling me that it's time to lie down and close my eyes."

It's important to be both firm and positive. If a child finds that limits are bent because of tiredness, the child may use being tired as an excuse later on. If a child feels blamed for being tired, then being sent to bed seems like a punishment. Instead, the message should be, "Right now you're tired. You're lucky you can go to sleep so you can get the rest you need."

It's a good idea to give warnings before bedtime so the child has a chance to finish playing. Then, be firm, "In a few minutes, I'm going to help you get ready for bed . . . Now it's time . . . I see you don't want to stop playing with those cards . . . They'll be here in the morning . . . Your eyes look tired. It's time to get some rest . . . Can you come by yourself or do you need me to help you?"

A pleasant bedtime routine can really help. At the Toddler Center, 16 children take naps every day. Each child has special time with a caregiver to get ready. The caregivers help the children take off their play clothes and change diapers, chatting all the while. Then, they say something like, "Do you want to get your blanket? Do you want to pick out a special stuffed animal to take with you? . . . Now lie down and I'll tuck you in. That soft blanket feels good, doesn't it? Do you want me to hold your hand as you fall asleep?"

Children have to slow down in order to get ready for sleep. It's a good idea to keep before bedtime activities calm rather than exciting. "The kids look so cute in their pajamas and are so sweet that my husband can't help playing with them," says one mother. "Pretty soon, he's swinging them around and getting them totally wound up. When he stops, we have a real job trying to get them to quiet down enough to go to sleep."

It helps to talk about what will happen after they sleep so our toddlers will have something to look forward to. "After your nap, you'll have a snack. And then your mom will come and get you."

For some children, it's a good idea to offer a special blanket, stuffed animal, or doll for comfort. It helps to have something to hold or talk to when we're not there. Other children may be afraid of the dark and a light can make a real difference. This could be a night light or a room light.

Whether the problem comes up at bedtime or in the middle of the night, it's important to decide ahead of time what to do with a child who won't stay in bed or who starts crying. The mother of two-year old Russell said, "It's after the hug and the kiss, and I've left the room that the trouble starts. At first, he's so charming. He comes padding out saying, 'I need to give you a bigger hug.' Then he rushes back to bed. But soon, he is calling 'Mommy, I need a drink.' A few minutes later it's, 'Mommy, I'm hungry!' Then, 'Mommy, I'm scared. I want you here.' If I don't stay, he cries or comes to get me."

As with setting any limit, the key is to decide what we want to do and then to be very consistent about doing it. This is hard unless we're in touch with our own feelings. Russell's mother remembers, "...having terrible nightmares when I was a child, so I rushed to be with Russell whenever he woke up crying, telling him he just had a bad dream. Pretty soon he stood up and yelled, 'Bad dream!' somewhere around 2 a.m. every night."

When all else fails, letting a toddler cry for a short time is not harmful. Some parents have no problem with this, but for others it's difficult. "I can't bear to let him cry alone in the room. He'll think I don't love him." When we're sure we've cared for our child's physical and emotional needs, staying firm about bedtime may be necessary. Some toddlers use crying at night to get extra attention from parents. They may cry just to get parents to do what they want. When this works, it can be a difficult habit to break.

If a parent finally decides to let a child cry, it's important to stick with it for at least a few days. The father of one-year-old Myra says, "I used to rock Myra to sleep every night, but it was taking longer and longer, and I wasn't getting any time to myself. The first night I decided not to do it, I carried Myra, kicking and screaming, to bed. She sobbed her heart out for over an hour. I kept returning to the room every fifteen minutes to let her know I was still there, even though she had to stay in bed. The next night, it took half an hour, and by the third night, Myra walked cheerfully to bed all by herself! I asked myself why I hadn't done it sooner."

If our toddlers just don't seem tired enough to fall or stay asleep, they may not be getting enough chances to be active. The mother of eighteen-month old Joshua says, "The woman who cared for Joshua as a baby liked to cuddle with him and read to him for hours. She didn't really enjoy taking him outside to the park. When I arranged for Joshua to be in a play group where he could run and play in the mornings, he became much more willing to go to bed at night."

If naps become a power struggle with the child, we can tell the child, "You don't have to go to sleep, but you do have to stay in bed and rest for awhile." A quiet time for everybody can be a real boost when we're the ones who are tired.

Sometimes we may need to adjust nap and bedtimes to fit into our own schedules. Parents who work all day may decide to keep their toddlers up at night to visit and let them take longer afternoon naps at their day care centers. Or children who need an earlier bedtime can be awakened earlier instead of being allowed to sleep late into the afternoon.

After a bedtime battle, it's a comfort to know

that sleeping will get easier as our children get older. They'll learn to recognize their own tiredness and will become more willing to rest. And a little experience can really payoff. "It was so satisfying," says the mother of two children. "I called my brother when his baby was about twelve months old. He'd tried everything, but his little boy kept fussing and wouldn't sleep. I suggested that he put the baby in his bed and come talk with me

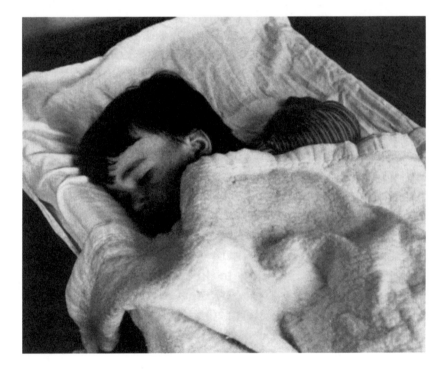

on the phone. After all, he'd tried everything else. I kept my brother on the phone for about 10 minutes. By the end of our talk, to his amazement, his little boy was fast asleep."

9

Saying Good-Bye is Sad

*I*T WAS ONE-YEAR-OLD *Jeffrey's second week at the Toddler Center. His father, Paul, lifted him from the car and gave him a tight hug. "Be a big boy for Daddy," he whispered, "and don't cry when I go. You cried every day last week. I feel so bad when you cry. Please, don't cry today."*

Jeffrey looked at the Toddler Center gate and burst into tears. He wrapped his arms and legs around his father, sticking like glue. Paul carried his wailing son through the gate, looking as if he might cry himself. He walked up to Jeffrey's caregiver, Wendy, and said sadly, "I don't know why Jeffrey gets so upset when I bring him here. And it seems to be getting worse."

Wendy smiled warmly. "Partly it's because he knows you're upset, and partly because crying is just his way of saying good-bye right now."

Paul hugged his little boy, who was still clinging tightly to him, but crying less loudly, and asked, "Could it be because he doesn't like being here? May be he's not old enough yet."

Wendy smiled again and said, "Jeffrey stops crying just a few minutes after you're gone and is happy most of the day. I think he's doing fine."

Suddenly Paul laughed. "I'm having a bigger problem than he has. It's awful, but I keep wishing I could trade with my wife. Let her do the dropping off and me do the picking up."

Hearing his father laugh, Jeffrey looked up to see what was going on. Wendy came close to Jeffrey and said, "I'm going to help your Daddy to say good-bye. He's sad, just like you are."

Jeffrey grabbed his father even more tightly and wailed. "No! No! No go!"

Wendy gently helped Paul peel his son off his body, saying to Jeffrey, "It's okay if you cry. I'll hold you as long as you need me. We'll go to the window and wave."

Paul walked quickly out the door, waved, and hurried off to work.

Saying good-bye is hard for almost everyone. Parents need to have time away from their toddlers, and it's also good for toddlers to be away from their parents. They learn that the separation doesn't last forever; their parents do come back. They learn they can trust and have fun with other adults. And finally, they start to feel strong and independent. They can be happy with other people too.

It's normal for parents to have mixed feelings about all this. Just ask any group of parents how they feel about leaving their toddlers:

"Guilty! Guilty! Guilty!"

"Once she was smiling when I left. I ran back for one last kiss and she burst into tears. I felt so ashamed. It was like I wanted to know that she'd miss me."

"If he can be so happy with other people, what does he need me for?"

"She's growing up so fast. It makes me feel proud and sad at the same time."

Like most child care programs, the Toddler Center has had a lot of practice in helping with goodbyes. One caregiver said, "I wish I could give a class on how to say good-bye. I'd tell parents how to make it easier on themselves and their toddlers. I'd tell parents to:

- Be clear that you're going to leave. Say, 'I'm going to work now. I'll see you after nap time.' If you want your child to trust you, don't try to sneak out. And don't ask for your child's permission. They have a choice about whether they cry, but not about whether you're going."

- Accept the sad feelings - yours as well as your child's. Don't make your children feel they are bad if they cry by asking them to 'be good and not cry.' In fact, it's fine if you tell them 'I feel sad too.' "

- Wait to leave until your child is really with a person. Make sure the caregiver can give your toddler full attention. Take a moment to tell the caregiver what's been happening like, 'Jessica might be hungry soon. She didn't eat her breakfast. She feels proud, though, because she put her shoes on all by herself.' "

- Make your good-bye short and matter of fact. Hug. Kiss. And move out the door. Stop and wave. And GO. It's okay to be sad, but if you hang around acting upset, your child will feel there's something wrong with you leaving and may get scared and much more upset."

The caregiver looked at the room of happily playing toddlers and laughed. "One more thing," she said, "I wish all the parents who left this morning had 'super' x-ray vision so they could see their children right now."

10

MINE!

"YOU'VE BEEN USING that pail all day, let Robin have a turn."

"No!"

"Don't you want to share it?"

"No!"

"Don't you want Robin to be happy?"

"No!"

The real meaning of sharing - giving of oneself - comes from inside. Toddlers are naturally self-centered. It's hard for them to think about other people's feelings.

Toddlers do not learn to share by having grown-ups make them do it. Having to give up a toy makes a toddler feel angry, not loving. At the Toddler Center, children play with toys until they're ready to give them up on their own. Caregivers may point out other toys, but they don't make them share or take turns. "I know it's hard to wait, but Dan is using that bike right now. You can find another bike over there."

It's harder at home, where there might not be more than one of each kind of toy. As parents, we may feel pressure to make our own children share, especially when another child is our guest. Davita's mother found a balance between respecting two-year old Davita's needs to be in charge of her own toys, and her own need to have visiting children feel comfortable. "Davita used to grab every toy a visiting child would even look at," she remembers. "Finally, I talked with her before another child came over. We put away the toys she wasn't willing to share. The first time, almost everything went into the closet. Then Davita found out it was more fun having toys to play with. Now, she only wants a few special things put away."

Without pushing our toddlers, we can talk

about the sharing we do ourselves. "I'm sitting on this chair, but I'm happy to share it with you." And we can pay lots of attention when children start to share on their own. "Wow, Scotty! You let P.J. look at that book with you. See how he's smiling?"

With no help from us, children will often do loving things for and with each other. Sharing a kiss or sharing a hug feels good. And this good feeling is what real sharing is all about.

11

Fighting . . . It's a Part
of Life Too

*I*N <u>YOUR CHILDREN SHOULD KNOW</u>, *a book about
stopping child abuse by Flora Colao and Tamar
Hosansky, one of the authors describes how she taught
her daughter to always act gently and kindly. The first
day her little girl was at preschool, another child hit her
and pulled her hair. Her daughter raised her hand to
hit back, then stopped herself, as she'd been told. She
looked up at her mother, puzzled and hurt, not knowing
what to do. The mother realized she'd prepared her
child to live in an ideal, peaceful world which doesn't
exist yet.*

Children need to know not only how to stop
themselves from fighting, but what to do when another
child picks on them. Just as it's normal for toddlers to
feel angry at times, it's normal for them to try dealing

with that anger by fighting. They're exploring the world, and they get in each others' way. They are also finding out the limits to what they can do to, or with, each other. Yelling, grabbing, pushing, and hitting are all part of this exploration.

When children fight at the Toddler Center, caregivers help them work out the problem for themselves, as long as they can do it without hurting each other. When Sally and Nick grabbed the same bucket they began to yell, "Mine! Mine!" Their caregiver, Carol, knelt down next to the two yelling children and said, "You're both pulling on that bucket. You both want it." Sally and Nick kept trying to pull the bucket away from each other, yelling louder and louder. Carol added in a calm, loud voice,

"I see you're both mad. You both want that bucket. There are more buckets over there." She pointed to the other buckets lying in the sandbox. Sally stopped yelling and looked to where Carol was still pointing. She ran to the sandbox and grabbed a bucket. Then she looked up at Carol with a big grin on her face, shouting "Bucket!" Carol smiled. "That's great, Sally. You found another bucket."

Adults in this situation often say things like:

"Sally had the bucket first. Nick will have to wait."

"Sally has had the bucket a long time. Nick needs a turn."

"I don't like fighting. I'm going to put the bucket away."

If Carol had taken over like this, the children would have lost a chance to learn how to work out things for themselves. At the same time, it was important that she be right next to the children. Then, for example, if Sally had started to push Nick to get the bucket, Carol would have put her arms around Sally gently, but firmly, and said. "Sally, I don't want you to push. You can be mad that Nick is grabbing that bucket, but I'm not going to let you push him. Tell him you're still using it; you can say 'stop.'"

In order to keep children from hurting each other, an adult needs to move close as soon as toddlers start to get angry. We want our toddlers to feel safe. They can yell or grab, but they need to know that we will always stop them from hurting or acting like they are going to hurt each other.

We can encourage our more timid toddlers to stand up for themselves. "You can say, 'No! My turn!'"

. . . You can hold tight with both hands . . . You didn't hold tight, and now Timmy has it . . . You can go and try to get it back . . . It looks like you don't want it right now . . . Sometimes it's scary when kids pull hard on toys."

Some children go through a time of testing when they will seem to grab everybody's toys and disrupt everybody's games. In this case, the child needs to be stopped and told. "I'm not going to let you take things from other children right now." If this behavior keeps happening, we may want to look at what might be behind the actions. Maybe the child is upset by a change of some kind. Talking things out with another person who knows the child can really help.

Sometimes children hurt each other, not because they mean to, but because they are curious about each others' bodies. When Becky grabbed a handful of Kim's shiny hair, Kim's mother pried her fingers loose and said, "Becky, you're very interested in Kim's hair. It's soft and shiny, isn't it? You can touch her hair gently like this." She stroked both children's heads. Becky reached again as if she were going to pull Kim's hair. Gently, Kim's mother stopped Becky's hand and said calmly, "Becky. I want you to touch Kim's hair gently." After a few tries, Becky stroked Kim's hair very gently.

Toddlers learn a lot from getting mad at each other and then working things out. They need adults close by to keep things from getting out of hand and to help them find words for their feelings and choices for their actions.

12

Biting

*E*IGHTEEN-MONTH-OLD KENNY STOOD *quietly, watching his four-year-old sister. It's possible to guess at the sort of thoughts going through Kenny's head. "I wonder about this girl here . . . I know what she looks like . . . I know what she feels like . . . I know what she smells like . . . But what does she taste like? . . . I'll just find out . . . Wow, she made a big noise! And she dropped that doll she never lets me play with . . . Uh oh! Looks like Mama's real mad at someone . . . Who? Me?"*

For most of us, biting is more upsetting than almost any other behavior our toddlers can try out. There's something animal-like about the idea of our toddlers chomping on one another.

But it's normal for most toddlers to bite at one time or another. They bite because they are curious.

Or because they are copying each other. They may bite if they're angry. Or when they are teething and feel like biting on something and another child just happens to be handy.

Some toddlers will test with their biting just as they will test with any other behavior. From their point of view, a lot of interesting things happen when they bite. The other child screams and drops the toy they want. An adult gets excited. Biting becomes a way of making things happen.

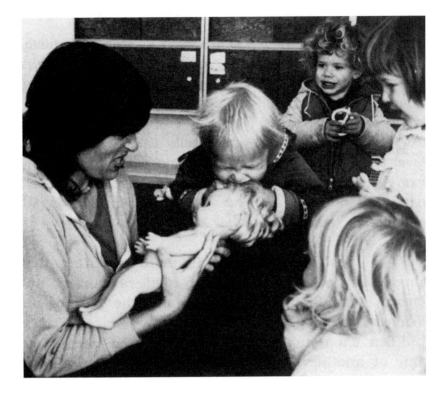

Caregivers have learned many ways to stop toddlers from biting at the Toddler Center:

- bites are stopped before they happen whenever possible. A caregiver always comes up close as soon as two children start to get mad at each other. If one child moves close to the other, mouth opened and teeth bared, the caregiver says loudly. "Stop! You're really mad, you want that toy. But I'm not going to let you bite."

- the children are given things that are okay to bite: toys, teething rings, food. If children try to bite a lot, they're offered a "chew toy" that they can bite on whenever they want.

- there's lots of talk about biting. How it feels good to our teeth. But not to other people. Pictures are shown of people sinking their teeth into all kinds of things - except each other.

When a child does bite, the caregiver says firmly, "Stop yourself. You bit Kelly and her arm hurts. She's crying. I don't want you to bite people. If you need to bite, you can use your chew toy." The caregiver comforts the child who was bitten, saying calmly. "That hurts. You and Julie both wanted that toy and she bit you." The bite is washed and disinfected. The caregiver acts calm rather than upset in order to keep things from being too interesting for the biter or the victim.

Dealing with a toddler hooked on biting is a real challenge. It takes a lot of careful watching and patience. After weeks of stopping Mikey from biting other children, his caregiver said, "Today, Mikey had an argument with Joey about who was going to go first on the slide. His mouth was open as if he might bite, but instead he yelled. 'Stop!' At last, we're getting through to him!"

13

Tantrums

"*G*ABRIEL AND *I had a perfect walk in the rain together. I felt like such a good mother. Then we got home and he got upset because I wanted to change his pants. He was soaking wet, and I told him he couldn't play until he was wearing dry clothes. He threw himself to the floor shrieking and lay there kicking, hitting, and shouting. I stood there wondering what I'd done to deserve this!*"

Sometimes toddlers completely lose control. This kind of behavior is often called a tantrum. There are lots of possible reasons: over-tiredness; too much excitement; being rushed when we're in a hurry; frustration over wanting to do more than they really can.

When Gabriel first started to get upset his mother could have reflected back to him what she saw happening: "You sound *really* mad. I know you want to wear those pants, but they're all wet." By giving him a chance to help find a solution, "Gabriel, do you want to wear these red pants or the blue ones?" she might have helped Gabriel avoid a full-blown tantrum.

Of course, this approach might not have worked. Sometimes, nothing we do or say will keep a child from becoming totally upset. In fact, our words may only get lost in the yelling. This is not a time when a child usually wants to be held. In this situation, we can give the toddler space to kick and cry, while making it clear that we won't let anybody get hurt. "You can lie on the pillows and kick, but I won't let you kick me." And we can let the child know what will happen when the upset behavior is stopped. "When you're finished screaming, we'll get some dry pants and you can go play."

Tantrums often happen at embarrassing places like a supermarket, a restaurant, or a friend's house. It can be tempting to give in to whatever the child wants, just to avoid a scene. Although we've all done this, it's a big mistake in the long run. If a toddler finds out that having a tantrum is a way around our limits, the child may start throwing tantrums all the time. As Gabriel's mother said, "I knew that I had something to do with Gabriel's tantrum. Last time we went to the store, Gabriel started screaming and I gave him a cookie to get him to stop." One way to handle a tantrum in public is to go to a more private place like the car or another room until things calm down.

Tantrums can leave parents frazzled and worn out. Kids bounce back more easily, "Just as quickly as it had started, Gabriel's tantrum was over. He picked out some dry pants and let me help him get them on. Then he ran cheerfully off to play, his eyelashes still wet with tears."

Parents whose children are having tantrums can remember that:

- it's important not to catch a child who throws tantrums by surprise. Instead, we can let children know ahead of time what is going to happen and what we will want them to do. Kids who know what to expect are less likely to have a tantrum.

- bending limits to avoid a tantrum will probably lead to more tantrums in the long run. When limits are enforced in a clear and consistent way, a child knows what to expect.

- children who are angry need to have their feelings acknowledged, accepted, and respected. If they're mad, let them *be* mad.

- adults do best to stay as calm as possible during a tantrum. A parent screaming at a screaming child will only make matters worse.

Young children grow out of becoming so upset that they lose control of their bodies. As they get older, they learn to use words to express feelings. They become able to do more for themselves and to find choices that work for them.

14

Wait Til I'm Ready
(Toilet Learning)

O N ONE SIDE, the "experts" are telling parents to be "Patient. Encouraging. Understanding. Calm." On the other side, grandparents, preschools, friends and even our own needs are pressuring us to hurry our toddlers with toilet learning.

"All of Sammy's friends are toilet trained. He's not even interested."

"My parents act like I'm doing something wrong by not pushing him. But my brother wet the bed until he was 12 years old. Was that any better?"

"I'm so tired of changing diapers. Will it never end?"

"She can't go to preschool until she's toilet trained, and she's so ready otherwise."

Most books and magazine articles are in agreement about toilet learning. They say things like:

"You can make yourself and your child miserable by trying, but you can't force children to use the toilet."

"Don't worry. Children want to do as others do. Your child won't go to college, or even kindergarten, wearing diapers."

"To use the toilet, children must have the ability to control their bodies and to understand the process with their minds. This can happen at very different ages with different children."

"Although some children learn earlier, most children become trained by day between two to three years old and by night between two-and-a-half to four-and-a-half years old."

It helps to compare learning to use the toilet with learning to do other things - like walking. We watched patiently while our babies struggled to crawl or creep along the floor, all on their own. When our babies started to pull themselves up, we held out hands to grab onto, pointed out couches to lean on, and let them know we were pleased. Some of our babies seemed to start walking overnight. Others went back and forth between crawling and standing, toddling and falling for months. However they did it, they were the ones in charge of learning to walk. We were there to help and to let them know that walking was something we were glad they were doing.

Toilet learning can work just the same way. We

can start by helping our children become aware of what their bodies are doing.

We can try talking about how good it feels to be clean. "Yes, that diaper was cold and sticky. Dry diapers feel better."

Not all children will agree with this. One little boy was annoyed every time his mother cleaned him. "No!" he'd grumble. "Mine!"

We can show our toddlers how other people use the toilet. Long before they're ready to try it themselves, most young children are fascinated by the toilet and what happens there. One mother had to warn her male visitors because her little boy dashed into the bathroom to watch them every time he got the chance.

At the Toddler Center, it's not uncommon to see one child, the star of the show, perched on the toilet, while other children sit all around, full of interest.

The time to start toilet learning is when our toddlers show signs of being ready, like:

- having dry diapers for longer periods of time.

- letting us know that they've pooped or peed in their diapers.

- showing interest in sitting on a toilet or potty chair wanting to wear underpants.

- disliking wearing wet or soiled diapers.

It's also important that this be a time when no other big changes are happening at home. Stress from a new baby arriving, changing child care, moving to a new home, or parents separating can make toilet learning much more difficult than it has to be. Stress can also cause a child who has been using the toilet to want to go back to diapers again.

Sometimes, for no clear reason, children who have been using the toilet for months will suddenly stop and want to wear diapers again. As with learning any new skill, it's normal for some children to need to go one step forward and two steps backwards. Sooner or later, they'll be ready to go forward again.

The more familiar the child is with the idea of using the toilet, the easier learning will be. Teaching the words we use for different functions and parts of the body makes the subject easier to discuss with our toddlers. It's a good idea to choose words that we feel most comfortable hearing out in public.

Other ways to prepare our toddlers include:

- reading books about using the toilet.

- letting them practice sitting on or trying to use the potty.

- making it easy by having them wear clothes they can take off - elastic waist pants rather than snap-on overalls.

- taking the child to pick out "your very own potty chair."

- talking about the time when "you won't need diapers and you can wear panties all the time like the big kids do."

For most parents, the process of their child's learning to use the toilet seems endless. We can make it easier by:

- staying relaxed. Too much excitement when a child "succeeds" can create almost as much pressure as showing disappointment when a child "fails." A pressured child becomes self-conscious and unwilling to try.

- realizing that it may take our time and energy to get our child "over the hump." "He trained himself when we were on vacation and could give him lots of attention. Besides, we were camping and he could go anywhere."

- having good communication with all the people who take care of our child so we all handle things the same way.

- having plenty of training pants. Some parents find it helpful to start with training pants only after their child has shown the ability to stay dry in diapers for long periods of time and has started using the toilet regularly.

- being prepared for extra laundry. Some parents choose to let the child wear few or no clothes much of the time. This may cut down on laundry. Waterproof pads and mattress covers can help keep bedding dry.

- knowing the location of all the public restrooms in town and being ready to get there in a hurry. "Why does he always have to go just as I've finally gotten to the front of a long line at the bank?" Some children are only willing to go at home. Instead of forcing them to sit on a strange toilet, it's better to wait until they feel more comfortable.

- being willing to find other places for them to use in emergencies besides bathrooms, especially when they're just learning.

- expecting that it will take a lot of time for our toddlers to perfect this new skill. Even older children sometimes have accidents, especially if they get cold or too involved in playing. Accidents are a time for calm cleaning up, not scolding or punishment.

It can take far longer for a child to gain control at night than during the day. It may help to cut down on liquids before bedtime, but some children sleep so deeply they just can't wake up. "Saul's doctor said not to worry until he was six years old. To cut down on laundry, we carried him to the toilet just before going to bed ourselves. He flopped like a limp rag doll, and never even woke up. This went on for a couple of years, until one night just after he turned five. When I went to pick him up, he opened his eyes, smiled at me, and walked to the toilet by himself. That was the end of it."

It's hard to be patient, but giving in to the temptation to push a child can cause real problems. "With Laurie, we felt a big need to get it over with," said one father. "We took her out of diapers as soon as she was two years old. We yelled at her whenever she had an accident. She became so upset that she tried not to go to the bathroom at all, and ended up getting so constipated we had to take her to the doctor. We just relaxed with our second child. It seemed like Marcie was going to be in diapers forever, but all of a sudden she trained herself with no trouble at all."

Toddlers grow in mind and body at very different speeds in very different ways. "I have to keep asking myself, what's the hurry?" said one mother. "He's running on his own clock. He'll get there when he's ready."

15

For Toddlers There's Only One Difference, and It's Really Very Small (Sex Roles)

"WHY DOES IAN have a barrette in his hair?" asked his mother when she came to pick up her little boy at the Toddler Center.

"He wanted one," explained his caregiver, Sue, "I'd given one to Laura and he asked for one too."

"It looks kind of strange for a boy to wear a barrette." worried Ian's mother.

"We offer barrettes to all kids here," replied Sue. "We want Ian to feel that he gets the same things as any of the other children."

It's important that young children believe that what they can do, or have, or feel is not dependent on whether they are girls or boys. When they're older, they can sort out differences like who really has the babies. Right now, we want our toddlers to feel good about themselves and to have the chance to grow into the most they can become.

Doing this is harder than it sounds. Without meaning to, it is really easy to tell boys that they must

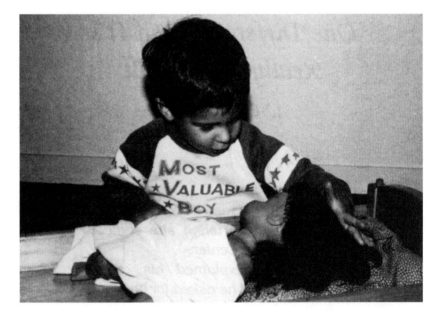

be strong and girls that they must be pretty. Of course, there's nothing wrong with being strong or pretty. It's just that there's more to life than only one or the other.

Treating girls and boys in an equal way means:

- Talking to a little boy about his caring behavior, not laughing at him. "Jerry, you're holding that doll so gently."

- Making sure that all children wear comfortable clothing and sturdy shoes. Frilly dresses don't protect little girls from scraped knees or cold weather. A child that wants to wear a frilly dress could always wear a pair of pants underneath.

- Talking to a little girl about what she does as well as how she looks. "See how fast you ran."

- Talking to a little boy about how he looks as well as what he does. "That hat from the dress-up box makes you look fancy."

- Letting little girls make big noises, "You can yell really loud!"

- Telling stories about men cleaning houses and women fixing things as well as the other way around.

- Saying to a crying child, "You're sad," not "Oh, what a poor little girl!" or "Big boys don't cry!"

Some children let other kids pick on them. All children - boys and girls - need to be able to stand

up for themselves. In our society, girls are more likely than boys to fall into a "victim role." At the Toddler Center, a conscious effort is made to help children learn to speak up for themselves rather than depend on an adult to jump in and rescue them.

Every day at the Toddler Center, Rosie stood sobbing while Zeke grabbed a truck away from her and ran to the other side of the yard. Every day her caregiver said, "You can find another truck, or you can try to get that one back." Rosie kept crying and came close to the caregiver, who said calmly, "I see you're upset that Zeke took your truck. When you're ready, you can let him know you're upset."

Finally, the day came that Rosie went after her truck. Zeke was so surprised that he almost dropped it into her hand. "Mine!" Rosie said firmly and marched away. Zeke followed after her. Rosie turned and glared at him. "Mine!" she said again. Zeke looked up at the caregiver standing nearby and decided that he might as well go dig in the sandbox.

In spite of all we do, we still have to find ways to deal with people who don't share our views about equality. One mother got fed up with strangers who kept gushing about her small daughter, "Oh, what a sweet, cute, little girl!"

"Yes," the mother answered, "She's also quite strong and very smart."

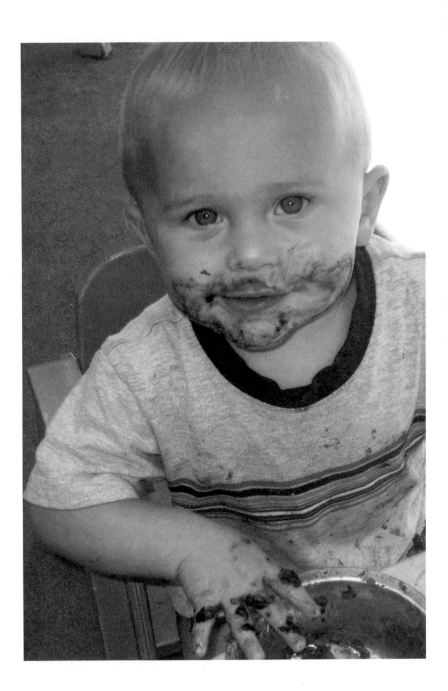

16

I Like to Eat . . . My Way

"*EAT! EAT!*" *WHINED 18-month-old Shelly, pounding the table, while her father, Peter, rushed to prepare her oatmeal.*

"I know you're hungry, and I'm doing the best I can!" sighed Peter. Then he added, "It's ready," and set a bowl of oatmeal in front of his daughter.

"Yuck!" said Shelly, pushing away the bowl.

"But you always eat oatmeal for breakfast," said Peter in a puzzled voice.

"Pasgetti" demanded Shelly.

"We had spaghetti last night," explained Peter. "Right now I made oatmeal for you and if you're hungry, that's what you're going to eat." He sat down and started to eat his own breakfast.

Shelly glared at him, then dumped her oatmeal onto the floor. "Shelly! Don't do that! Your breakfast is over!" yelled Peter. Then, rushing to clean things up, he muttered to himself, "I'm going to be late for work. My coffee's cold. I hope she's not going to get too hungry. Well, I guess she can eat something at her child care."

At mealtimes, our toddlers' wishes and our own are often in conflict.

> Toddler: Hungry!
> Parent: But you wouldn't eat anything just half an hour ago.

> Toddler: I don't want that!
> Parent: But I made it just for you.

> Toddler: Cookie!
> Parent: You need healthy food.

> Toddler: Watch me!
> Parent: Just for once. It'd be nice to have peace and quiet while I'm eating. Or maybe a little adult conversation.

By working out a balance between children's needs and parents' needs, meals can become a time of learning and fun rather than a battleground. It helps to keep in mind that:

- toddlers will eat when they're hungry, but might not eat much. It makes sense to offer only simple, healthy food like apples, bananas, oatmeal, eggs, whole grain bread, cheese, and cooked vegetables such as broccoli and carrots. We can serve whole grain crackers, cookies and chips rather than the more processed and less nutritious kind. Giving very small servings cuts down on wasted food and lets toddlers have a chance to ask for more.

- toddlers need to eat more often than we do. Their stomachs are smaller. Their bodies are more active. Some parents have food available all the time. Others offer meals or snacks every two to three hours on a regular schedule.

- toddlers like to have choices. Bread or crackers, eggs or oatmeal, an apple or an orange. "At breakfast, I give him a choice before I make it," says one mother. "But once it's made, that's it - he can't change his mind."

- toddlers may not like the same foods we do. Young children may find the lasagna we so lovingly prepared to be too spicy. While we shouldn't force them to eat it, we also don't want to be preparing two dinners. It's a good idea to keep healthy, easy alternatives on hand, like cereal and milk.

- toddlers love to be part of the action. They're messy eaters who spill and drop a lot. So their eating place had better be easy to clean up.

- food made easy to eat with a spoon or fingers lets toddlers feed themselves. "He loves it when I let him make his own food," says one father. "He works very hard at spreading the peanut butter on his rice cracker. Of course, I have to be right there to keep track of the peanut butter jar."

Meals can be a time for conversation with our toddlers. Since young children may not say many words, it's important for us to pay attention to what they try to show us as well as to the words they use. When Ben reached toward his father with a gooey hand, his father said, "You're reaching with your hands, Ben. Do you want more macaroni and cheese?" Ben nodded his head.

We can talk in a positive way, letting our toddlers know what we do want instead of what we don't want. For example, "Lift up your arms so I can clean the table," instead of "Get your hands off the table." Or "There are two chairs here. You can pick which one you want to sit on" instead of "Get in your chair!" Rather than scolding children for spilling, we can point out what happened and start over. "Your milk fell over . . . It's okay . . . Here's a sponge to clean up the table. Can you help me push it? We'll clean up the floor later. I'll pour you more milk."

And we can still set limits:

- "I want you to put your book down when you

eat, Nicole. I can put it next to me or you can put it on that table. It will be there when you've finished eating."

- "I don't like it when you dump out your milk, Roger. I'll put your cup away for now."

- "When you're yelling, Leslie, I can't understand what you want . . . Oh, more eggs. Sure!"

- "Matt, I need you to keep your plate on the table. I don't want it to fall off."

When a child gets interested in playing instead of eating, we can decide the meal is over. "You're looking at your blocks, Ann. Does that mean you're done? Can you hand me your cup?" Or "You keep getting up from the table, Leo. If you leave the table again, I'm going to end your lunch."

It's difficult to have an adult conversation during a meal with a toddler. Young children tend to do things at meals that interrupt everything else that's going on. Adult and older (school-aged) children in a family may want meals that are not toddler-oriented, especially at dinner time. In many families, the toddler has an early dinner and the other members eat later so they can have a chance to talk with each other. The toddler may sit with the rest of the family for a while, but not eat much or stay long. Other families let the meals be very informal, but set aside other times for adult conversation.

Toddler Centered Meals

Mealtime at the Toddler Center is a little like a three ring circus. Three low horseshoe shaped tables, five or six toddlers sitting in little chairs around the outside, eating and talking, one caregiver sitting on the inside, very busy but very calm. Each table has a huge pile of cloth wipes, a pitcher full of warm water and a bowl for rinsing. Meals are served outside whenever the weather permits. Caregivers start with a song, which brings the kids running. No high chairs are used, so the children have a choice about whether or not they want to be at the table. Only children sitting at the table eat.

There's lots for each toddler to do, see, and talk about. "Can you pick out a chair and bring it to the table? . . . Do you want a blue cup or a red one? ... Here comes the food! ... Put your cup down so I can pour the milk ... Oh, look at the apple! It's big and red! I'll cut it. Yes, the knife goes chop! chop! chop! . . . See, it has hard seeds. I'll take them out."

"Here are the bananas (there is a chorus of 'nanas!') Who wants to help me pull the peel off? . . . Now I'll cut up the banana . . . The banana has little soft seeds . . . Yes, we can eat these seeds . . . do you want banana or apple?"

"What's in the hot dish? . . . Oh look, eggs! Smells yummy . . . Can you push your bowl toward me? . . . Yes, your eggs are all gone! Do you want more? . . . If you're done you can give me your bowl . . . Come and get a wipe for your hands and face . . . Can you wipe it yourself or do you want me to do it for you? . . . All clean! . . . Now, you can go and play."

17

The Invaders From
Inner Space
(New Brothers and Sisters)

"*W*E TALKED WITH *Elaine so much about the new baby, I thought she'd be glad it was finally here. But when we got home from the hospital, she took one look at the baby in my arms and shouted, 'NO! NO! NO!'*"

Having a new baby in the family is hard on toddlers. Suddenly they have to share the most important thing in their lives - the love and attention of their parents. It would be strange if they didn't feel resentful at times.

Parents have plenty of ideas about how to help toddlers get used to the new baby:

- "I took her to see a friend's new baby so she'd know what to expect."

- "We read a lot of books about having new babies."

- "I let him help me. He hands me a diaper or brings me a new toy to show the baby."

No matter how much we try to prepare ourselves and our children, a new member of the family turns our world upside down. As one mother of two said, "I'd forgotten how much work there is with a new baby. And I'm so tired." It's important to make regular times to be alone with our toddlers, even for a few minutes, to let them know that they're still special. Each child needs these private times with each parent. In some families, it takes a conscious effort to keep the older child from becoming "Daddy's" and the newborn "Mommy's".

We can also help our toddlers sort out their feelings towards the new baby. Their love and excitement are likely to be mixed up with jealousy and the fear of being left out. "His favorite game was for me to pretend that I was the kid and to say all kinds of awful things about the baby. Then he'd switch and want to play being the baby himself and curl up on my lap with a blanket and a bottle."

No matter how much talking and play acting we do, our toddlers may need to show hurt and anger again and again. Some young children just have a harder time accepting a new baby than others. Feelings about a new baby might stay for a long time. The mother of three-year-old Juanita said. "It sounds funny, but much as I wanted this baby, I felt sad for Juanita. She would no longer be the only child. It was as if I were reliving the sadness I had after my sister came, when I was just about Juanita's age."

Caregivers at the Toddler Center often see a dramatic change in children's behavior upon the arrival of a new sister or brother. Soon after her brother was born, two-year-old Carmen started to demand adult attention in ways she never had before, like pushing other children out of her caregiver's lap. After noticing this, the caregiver made a time when she could sit alone with Carmen and say, "I know there's a lot going on at home right now with your new baby. Even though they spend time with the baby, your mom and dad love you a lot. And the Toddler Center is still your special place, and you're important to all of us." Then she cuddled with Carmen on her lap until Carmen was ready to get up and play.

While toddlers will have ups and downs with their brothers and sisters all their lives, the beginning is the hardest. "At first," said one mother, "having two children seemed like ten times as much work as having one. Stacy would want to sit on my lap just as Justin was nursing. Or Justin would start to cry just as I was reading Stacy a book. But now, they play together so happily so often that I'm really glad they have each other."

18

Out in Public

"I TRIED EVERYTHING." said the mother of two-year-old Roy. "But Roy just couldn't control himself in the store. He climbed out of the cart. He pulled things off the shelves and screamed when I took them away from him. I let him bring his own toys, but he threw them on the floor. I'd take him out of the store to get him to calm down, but he'd start acting up again as soon as we went back in. So, for a few weeks, I did the shopping without him at night, when a friend could take care of him. Then we tried again. He was fine. He even helped in the check-out line by handing things to the cashier! He thought that was great."

Whether it's a trip to the store, a meeting, or a visit with a friend, being out in public with toddlers often means bringing them to places that aren't set up for them and hoping they'll be "good". Dealing with new places and people is hard work for many toddlers. Like Roy's mother discovered, sometimes the best solution is to keep the child out of the situation awhile, and try again later.

This may be true even when the visit happens in our own houses. Toddlers don't like change. They do like having our full attention. "It was so frustrating!" Amy's mother explained. "My friend Beth came over to visit and every time we started to talk, Amy would interrupt us. She'd whine, hang on me, and start doing things I'd have to stop, like tearing up books. The more embarrassed and upset I felt with Amy, the worse she was. By the time Beth left, I was worn out. Next time, we'll get together when Amy's having her nap."

Most of the time, though, we can help our toddlers handle visits well by accepting their needs and planning around them. It's not fair to expect them to sit quietly like little adults with nothing to do but watch. Instead, we can make sure there are things for them to do.

Every week, Sandra visited with her uncle in the nursing home while her small daughter played happily in the corner. Even though little Corinne was just under two years old, she was very content to stay on her special blanket. Each week, she kept busy eating from her lunchbox, playing with toys, drawing pictures, and looking at books.

"Our visit is over." said Corinne's mother on

one occasion. "Thank you for taking such good care of yourself. Are you ready to go to the beach?"

"I busy," said Corinne, smiling impishly, "I visiting my crayons." She turned her back on her mother and went on coloring.

"How do you get Corinne to play by herself so well?" asked one of the nurses. "I could never have done this with my kids at her age."

"It takes a lot of planning and preparation, said Sandra. "To start with, I arrange to be here in the morning when Corinne is fresh and more able to be on her own. Then I get up early and take a long walk with her before we come. Otherwise, she'd never be able to sit still. I keep a bag of toys that she only gets to use when we're visiting, so she has something special to do. I tell her what to expect. She picks out her blanket, books, and food. And she knows that she can look forward to doing something fun with me after taking care of herself. It's worth all the effort because my uncle gets such joy out of seeing Corinne, even if he's not up to playing with her."

"But she's so happy for so long," said the nurse.

"It had to be very short visits at first," Sandra explained. "We worked up from there . . . Are you ready to go to the beach now, Corinne?"

Corinne put her crayons down, jumped up, and ran to her mother. "All done!" she shouted. "BEACH!"

Part Two

Successful Parenting

*A*T AN OFFICE party for a first time expecting mother, the experienced parents just had to offer a few words of advice.

"Make time for yourself while you can. After the baby is born, your whole life will change!"

"No matter what you do, there will come a day when your child will tell you that you've done it all wrong."

The future mother was starting to look worried. After all, she couldn't back out now. But then an older father added gently, "Being a parent is a heck of a job . . . and I wouldn't have missed it for anything in the world." Everybody nodded in agreement.

We are legally responsible for our children's care and actions for eighteen years. We may *feel* responsible for the rest of our lives. Raising children is a BIG JOB!

It helps to remember that, just as there are no perfect people, there are no perfect parents or children. There are no perfect families either, even if they look that way from the outside. It's not our job to be perfect, but to do the best we can.

Our job as parents can be easier if we help ourselves in the ways described in the following chapters.

19

Learn From Others

"**O**UR ONE-YEAR-OLD BOY *hunts down bugs and swallows them whenever he gets the chance. Crickets, snails, ants. At the same time, he turns up his nose at the food I give him. I thought maybe he had a nutrition problem, but his doctor said not to worry about it. I did worry, until the nurse in the doctor's office said that her boy had done the same thing. He finally grew out of it. Years later, when she took her son to a French restaurant for his graduation, he was ready to eat anything on the menu, except the escargots and frog's legs, which he now called 'gross.'*"

Somebody ought to write a song for parents of toddlers titled, "My Child Does That Too." It helps a lot to know that many things our children do have nothing to do with how well we're doing as parents or with how they'll turn out when they grow up.

We're lucky to be able to learn from other peoples' experiences in many different ways. We can:

- read books which tell us what children are like at certain ages and what other people have found to be helpful. (See resource section at the end of this book.)

- go to classes set up for parents of toddlers. These are offered through community colleges, adult education programs, hospitals, and parks and recreation departments.

- visit a toddler care center for a few hours and watch what goes on. After visiting for an afternoon, one father said, "I didn't know how well off I was! Some other kids are even more stubborn than my little girl. It was interesting to see how the teachers got them to do things anyway."

- ask family and friends for their suggestions. "I'd been so annoyed with my mother for all the pressure she'd been putting on me about toilet training that I was sure there wasn't a thing she could teach me. But when I thought my two-year-old boy just had a very bad cold, she said it might be pneumonia and to take him to the doctor. She was right. Even if we don't agree about everything, I'm glad to have a mother who cares enough to say what she thinks."

- ask the people who take care of our children. They see our toddlers in a different setting where they may have found other ways of dealing with day to day issues. "I couldn't figure out why Jessie liked to go to bed at her child care center but not at home" said Jessie's mother. "Finally, I asked her teacher. He said that they put Jessie's special blanket away at the Center, rather than letting her carry it around all day. That way she's glad to have the chance to have it at nap time. I tried doing this, and would you believe it, now bedtime for Jessie at home has stopped being a problem."

No one is born knowing what it's like to be a parent. Instead of doing everything the hard way by trial and error, we can save ourselves time and worry by learning from others. Less time and worry means more time for ourselves and more fun with our toddlers.

20

Trust Yourself

A S IMPORTANT AS it is to learn from others, trust your own thoughts and feelings about your child. No child is the same as yours. No one will know your child the way you do. You can get good ideas from others, but there is no one right answer for all children all the time. Beliefs about the best way to raise children go back and forth and around from time to time, place to place, and family to family. In our society, beliefs have ranged from "children should be seen and not heard" to "children should be free to do whatever they want" to "children need adults to set limits for them."

We need to stand by what we believe and stick up for our kids. This can be hard with people we know well, especially at their houses or if they have strong opinions of their own. Molly thought her friendship with Patty might be over the day she took her daughter, two-year-old Kristin, to visit Patty and her two-year-old son, Adam. When the two children began to pull on Adam's new stuffed giraffe, Molly started to get up. "No, wait," Patty said very firmly. "I read somewhere

that it's better to let them work it out completely by themselves. We shouldn't interfere at all."

Molly watched. After all, it was Patty's house. Besides, Patty had read more books about children than she had. Both children kept pulling on the giraffe until they were shrieking and crying, "Keep waiting," Patty said, "This is how they learn."

But when Adam and Kristin started to push and hit, Molly couldn't stand it anymore. "This can't be right," she told her friend. She sat down on the floor between the children and said firmly, "I see that you both really want that giraffe. I'm not going to let you push or hit each other to get it. You can play with it together. Or find another toy. But no hurting."

"Giraffe!" said Kristin.

"Mine!" said Adam.

"Kristin", said Molly, "Adam doesn't want you to have his giraffe right now. Adam, are there other toys in your room that you'd like to let Kristin play with?"

"Train!" shouted Adam, and the two children ran off to his room.

Molly kept sitting on the floor, not looking at her friend. To her surprise, Patty said, "That was wonderful. Why didn't you step in sooner?"

"Because I thought you'd be angry," explained Molly. "You sounded so sure you were right. Besides, this is your house."

"Let's agree to speak up right away when we disagree," said Patty. "And, when it comes to our kids, whose house it is doesn't matter."

Molly smiled, "What about that book you read?"

"I do get a lot of good ideas from books, but maybe I got this one mixed up. The way you helped work that out didn't really seem like interfering. You just helped them solve a problem," Patty laughed. "Anyway, it's interesting to try out new ideas. But it's even more important to look at what's really happening with our kids, and then trust our own thoughts and feelings."

And What About Relatives?

It's a fine line to walk. Our toddlers' grandparents, aunts, uncles, and cousins have rights, too. They love our children and, just as we do, want what's best for them. However, our relatives may have very different ideas than we do about what "best" means. It is possible to stick with what we feel is right for our children without attacking the other person's point of view.

UNCLE: When I was little, I had my mouth washed out with soap for saying those kinds of words.

PARENT: That's one way of doing it. I haven't chosen to do it that way.

GREAT AUNT: I made a special trip to the same candy store I used to take you to and got a big surprise for Tony.

PARENT: Isn't it thoughtful that you brought all these beautiful chocolates! What nice memories this brings back! I'm going to put the box up here for now. After dinner, you can surprise Tony, and help him pick out one piece.

GRANDMA: Haven't you toilet trained that poor
child yet? You're harming Gina by
letting her wear diapers at night.
PARENT: I spoke to Gina's doctor about it. She
says everything is just fine.

We do need to be flexible. The world is full of
all kinds of people, and it's good for our children
to get used to different ways of doing things.

"At Grandpa's house, you can't go into the living
room without an adult. It's full of things he doesn't
want to get broken. Yes, I know that's different from
the way we do it at home."

"At Aunt Esther's house you get to watch lots of
TV. Not at our house."

For most of us, our relatives are an important
part of our lives. It takes time to figure out how to
deal with their suggestions and pressure in ways we
can feel good about. As Charlie's father said, "I love
my folks a lot, but I was sick of being nagged. You'd
have thought I was the worst parent in the world!
It got so far that I didn't like to visit them, which
wasn't how I wanted to feel at all. Finally, I realized
that my parents have a big need to be part of what's
going on with Charlie. I started asking them to do
things with him that I remember as being special
when I was a kid. Playing games. Telling stories.
Now, when they want to give advice, I let them know
when I've heard their opinion. If they keep nagging,
I remind them that, even if I don't do some things

the way they did, I'm bound to do a good job raising my kid because I had *them* as parents. The more comfortable I've become in doing this, the more I've enjoyed my parents for the loving and interesting people they are."

21

Take Care of Yourself

WHEN KATY RETURNED from a weekend conference, it was clear that her two children had had a wonderful time. Lea, the young woman taking care of them is a preschool teacher with no children of her own. She had kept them busy and happy every minute they weren't asleep.

"I'm so tired," Lea said, "I'm sorry about not doing the dishes. And the room's a mess. The kids wanted my attention all the time. I could barely get their food made, and it's hard to find things that would interest both a two-year-old and a five-year-old for so long. How do you do this every day?"

Katy laughed. "It sounds like you never took a rest. I didn't expect you to play with them every single minute."

"Well, that's what I do at the preschool," Lea said.

"Preschool is just for a few hours," Katy pointed out, "and you have lots of help." She smiled fondly at Lea and explained gently, "I didn't hire you to teach preschool for the whole weekend. It was great for the kids, but much too hard on you. I hired you to act as their parent, and parents have to take time off for themselves. No parent could keep up the pace you did with the kids and still get all the household chores done."

"How do you take time off without making the kids unhappy?" asked Lea.

"It depends," said Katy. "Sometimes they play nicely together. Sometimes I can put them each on their own beds with some books and toys, and have them take a quiet time. Sometimes I just have to let them be unhappy. And sometimes, thank goodness, I can turn on Sesame Street."

Being a parent is at least an 18-year-long job. We're on-call 24 hours a day. If we don't take good care of ourselves, we'll never make it. Taking care of ourselves means:

- getting enough rest, exercise, and healthy food.

- time off to do fun things for ourselves.

- having interests outside of our children. Our children are an important part of our life, but should be free from the burden of being our whole life. It's healthy for our children to see us having interests besides our families.

- letting ourselves have grumpy days sometimes. That's part of real life too. Our kids will survive an angry word now and then. We can try to remember to explain our feelings later.

- learning how to relax and accept our imperfect selves and our imperfect children.

It helps to have support from family and friends. Some of us are lucky and have people close by to share feelings and child care with. The rest of us will have to find people.

Carla, who has a full time career, was the only person among her circle of friends to have a baby. "It was hard at first," she remembers. "There wasn't a person I could talk to. After I had called the doctor seven times in the first three days I was home, he suggested I go to a class for parents of infants. I did and became friends with a couple of the mothers there. I even stopped a woman who walked by our house every day with her baby, and got to know her. Now I have friends with whom I can share my life as a parent."

Single parents have to work even harder at taking care of themselves. Eva, a divorced mother of two, said, "After Fred left us, I was a wreck. I felt like my life was over. But I looked at my kids and saw how much they needed me, especially with their father gone. I had to pull myself together. I went to counseling and made some friends. It's still hard without a partner to share things with, but having support from others and a little time to myself has made a world of difference."

In our busy lives, it takes planning to find time for ourselves. Some ideas are to:

- set up an afternoon "quiet hour" each day,

even if our toddlers don't take naps. Once they're used to the idea, young children can happily entertain themselves. With children in bed with books or toys, parents have a chance to rest, visit on the phone with a friend, or get caught up on work.

• use times when our children are asleep for activities that are hard to do when they're awake. [One mother got up extra early for many mornings to write this book!]

• make sure we get out alone to do something fun at least once a week. This doesn't have to cost any money. Parents can have free child care by trading through a babysitting co-op, barter network, or arrangements with neighbors or friends. Activities might include taking long walks, browsing in a bookstore, or joining a discussion group.

• have a routine for what happens when we get home after being out at work all day. First, we need to spend at least a short time with our kids. After all, they've been away from us for hours. Then we can bring out a project for our toddlers while we take time for ourselves. Some parents keep special toys like building blocks or materials like play dough put away just for this purpose.

Children learn by example. When they see us being good to ourselves and enjoying life, they're far more likely to do the same.

22

Keep Your Child Safe

Toddlers are innately vulnerable due to their young age and small size. Furthermore, their drive towards independence and lack of life experience often puts them in danger.

Being constantly anxious is not the answer. As one father said, "I get so worried that I want to lock myself and my little boy in the house and not go out until he's 18 years old and we both have black belts in karate. But really, what kind of life would that be?"

No matter how hard we try, we can't protect our children from all the bad things that might happen to them. Not everything is under our control. And we have to take some risks in order to be able to enjoy life. By taking charge of their safety, we can protect our toddlers most of the time.

Thank you to Kidpower for permission to include content from their program in this chapter. For more information, see 'About the Author' or visit www.kidpower.org.

We can use our eyes and ears to keep track of what's going on every minute. Toddlers need our help to stay out of trouble. They'll try to find out what something feels or tastes like even if it's an electrical cord or the bleach bottle on our friend's laundry room floor. They'll dash to the other side of the street even if a car is coming. "We stopped at a garage sale," said one shaken father. "I turned my back for only a second, and my two-year-old son ran down the driveway. His sister grabbed him just before he went into the street, as a bunch of cars raced by. It's scary! What if she hadn't been there? Next time, I'll hold on to him every minute."

We can follow basic safety rules. Make children use their car seats every single time, even if they don't want to. Take toddlers out of the bathtub every time you go to answer the door or the phone, even if you plan to be gone "just a minute." Lock up poisons and sharp knives. And, never leave young children alone in a public place.

As one woman said, "After shopping, I saw a little boy asleep in the car next to mine in the parking lot. I really had to leave, but the child was too young to be left alone. Anyone might have come along. So I waited by the car, watching the little boy, until his mother came ten minutes later. She apologized, saying the line in the store was longer than she expected. I wanted to shout at her, "Your child is too young and too important to be left here even for a second!"

When there's the shadow of a doubt, check things out. Even in the most "child-proofed" areas, toddlers can find creative ways to get hurt. "It was the silence that made me wonder," said 18-month-old Kali's mother. "Usually, there's a little noise, but suddenly it was absolutely quiet. I went into Kali's room and found that she'd somehow gotten a fork and used it to pry the cover off the electrical outlet. I stopped her as she was about to poke the fork into the outlet."

Protecting Toddlers From Bullying, Abuse, and Abduction

As babies, toddlers, and preschoolers become more independent and move on their own out in the world, parents often worry about how to support their children in being safe with other people.

Some parents worry because their children are "too shy" and act anxious and withdrawn around people they don't know well. Other parents worry because their children have no discretion and will treat everyone as their new best friend. Some parents worry that their children will be so eager to please that they might be dominated by others. Other parents worry that their children will push against the boundaries of both peers and adults.

Children learn about boundaries from their adults, at a very young age. We need to set a good example by having clear personal boundaries ourselves and using our understanding of these boundaries in our interactions with our children. Even if a baby doesn't understand, he or she will respond to stress, tone of voice, and body language.

As soon as they can move around and begin to understand, children can be coached in learning about boundaries. Start with noticing and appreciating what each child CAN do and then build from there.

A crawling baby who wants to pet a cat needs close supervision as she is coached verbally and physically to "be gentle". Children can learn to "be gentle" when touching anyone. Even at young ages, children need to start to learn about NOT touching sometimes. You don't touch the stove because it's "HOT!" You can jump on Daddy, but not when he's ill. Many things are okay to touch, but NOT put in your mouth.

As they develop more speech and understanding, toddlers can start to use very simple skills and phrases to protect their own boundaries by saying, for example:

- "Stop."
- "I don't like that."
- "Move away."
- "I need space."
- "I'm using that"

Being polite by acknowledging people socially is an adult need, not a child's. We believe that younger children should not have to engage socially with adults until they feel ready. Children can learn to greet an adult when you say it's okay by making eye contact, waving, shaking hands, and saying, "Hello" or "Good-bye." However, this should be suggested gently rather than forced. If a child finds greeting new people to be difficult, the best plan is to model the behavior yourself and to let the child decide to greet others in his or her own way at his or her own pace.

If an adult is a family member or close friend, you might need to explain to this person that the rule in your family is that children don't have to hug or kiss anyone or sit on anyone's lap unless they want to.

Children get a very mixed message about their personal boundaries when they are pressured to be affectionate. Any form of touch or games for play, fun, or affection should be safe, the choice of each person, allowed by the grownups in charge, and never a secret.

The mother of two-year-old Wes found that upholding a child's right to refuse affection can be hard to do. "I had to tell my aunt to stop asking Wes to give her a kiss. To her it was kind of a game, but he really didn't like it. Her feelings were hurt for a long time, even though I explained that I didn't want Wes ever to feel that he had to give affection just because an adult said so."

As adults, we need to know that most of the people who harm children are people they know. The good news is that good supervision and strong boundaries can prevent most abuse.

Some important guidelines are:

• Children's bodies are important and

deserve to be treated with love and respect. Help them to stop unwanted tickling, roughhousing, teasing, or affection, by teaching them to say, "Stop!" and then respecting their requests. As children get older, start to teach them the safety rules about private areas. Most toddlers are too young for this to make sense to them.

- Some things, especially issues concerning health and safety, are not a choice. Whether they like it or not, we need to hold children's hands when crossing the street until they are old enough to cross safely on their own.

- Teach young children not to keep secrets. Many two year olds are old enough to understand that "There are no secrets from mom and/or dad". Secrecy is a major reason that child abuse can continue.

- Practice respectful listening to your toddler. Letting our toddlers know that we are here to listen can make a huge difference. When they try to tell us something, we can stop what we're doing and pay attention. By having that kind of relationship with us now, they'll be far more likely to come to us later if they need help.

The reality is that adults are often busy and

distracted - and children do need to learn to wait if they want something. However, even young children can be encouraged to be persistent in interrupting a busy adult if they have a safety problem.

We can teach young children about these boundary rules by using toys or puppets to act out different safety problems and solutions. We can have them practice in simple games. Make these practices fun rather than scary. For example, the safety problem can be another child or puppet gently pulling the child's hair rather than an adult doing something upsetting.

To keep our toddlers safe, we must only leave them with people we really trust and keep track of where they are all the time. Our children are too small and too precious for us to leave their safety to chance.

23

Help Your Child Face Grief and Loss

*W*HEN THREE-YEAR-OLD SASHA'S mother, Eleanor, came home from a night meeting, her friend, Jan, met her at the door. "Am I glad you're back!" Jan said. "Sasha cried from the moment you left! I couldn't get her to go to bed, so finally I just let her play in her room until she went to sleep. Come and have a look."

Puzzled, Eleanor walked with her friend into her daughter's room. Sasha had piled everything she owned onto her bed. Blocks, cars, books, dolls, even some clothes. Then she had climbed on top of the heap, snuggled into an impossible position, and fallen asleep.

Eleanor stroked her daughter's cheek, crouched down, and quietly started to put away the toys. "How strange," she whispered to Jan. "Sasha has never done anything like this before. And she's *always been so happy to stay with you."*

"A lot must be going on in her head right now," Jan whispered back. "The divorce has turned her world upside down. From Sasha's point of view, her father keeps disappearing. Maybe she's afraid other people and things she cares about will also disappear."

"Sasha sees her father every weekend," Eleanor protested.

"That's still a big change from seeing him every day," Jan pointed out.

"I hate thinking about Sasha having to go through all this," Eleanor sighed. "Maybe we should have waited to get our divorce until she was older and could understand things better."

"It would have been worse for Sasha to live with two people who were both so unhappy," Jan said. "She's upset now, but we can help her get through it. In the long run, she's better off seeing you feel good about your life."

No matter how much we want to, we can't always protect our children from loss and pain. Young children are affected strongly by big events such as a move to a new home, illness, divorce or separation of their parents, or the death of a person or pet they love. They need our help to deal with their feelings of grief and anger over these changes in their lives.

Most small children living through big changes don't have the words to tell us how they're feeling.

Toddlers often show their feelings in confusing ways, like going back to behaviors they've outgrown. They remember the younger age as a time when they were taken care of. Acting younger helps them feel safe.

Ways a toddler might show distress could be:

- loss of appetite.

- crying spells.

- nightmares.

- outbursts of anger.

- clinging.

- trouble going to sleep.

- bed wetting (if a child has been trained).

- being extra quiet.

- trouble saying good-bye.

The challenge is to "decode" these outward symptoms so we can figure out what is going on inside our toddlers. Then we can try to talk about what's happening and give them simple words for their feelings. We can show them by our tone of voice and the way we touch and hold them that they are loved.

A child's grief is painful for adults to face. It's tempting to deny what's going on, especially if this is how we were taught to handle grief when we were children. "When Gina's goldfish died," says her mother, "I felt at first that the fuss she made was ridiculous.

Then a picture popped into my mind of years ago, when my hamster died. I remember my mother saying, 'Don't make such a fuss!' But I felt so alone being so upset and having no way to share it. Gina and I had a wonderful talk about how her goldfish was her special friend and how sad she was that it was gone. Then we cried together, and we both felt much better."

It's normal for parents to feel worried and angry by some ways that children show grief. "Jeff started to suck his thumb again after the baby was born," said Jeff's father. "I really wanted to yell at him. I was afraid that if we let him get away with this now, he'd probably still be sucking his thumb in high school!"

Bess, a marriage and family therapist, had another point of view. "Thumbsucking is helping Jeff feel safe right now. The new baby means Jeff has lost his old place as the only child in his family. He needs help and comfort while finding his new place. If Jeff can work through these needs now, he'll be able to go forward with his life. It's the children whose needs are denied and pushed away who get stuck doing babyish things over and over."

If parents are upset by a situation, it's hard to give the extra energy to help the children cope. When Dora learned her husband had a heart condition, she couldn't face the fears of her three young sons on top of her own. The children's behavior became more and more out of control. Finally, Dora cried, "If you care so much, why are you being so bad?" With help from a counselor, Dora and the children were able to work out their feelings.

Children who've experienced loss often have fears it might happen again . . . or to them. It helps if we can put ourselves into our children's shoes, and imagine what their feelings might be. It's important to bring these fears out into the open. When Jewell was afraid to be away from her parents, her mother said, "Mommy and Daddy aren't going to go away forever like Grandma did. We have to go to work, but we'll come back. Grandma didn't want to leave you, but she was very old and it was time for her to die. Mommy and Daddy aren't old. And you aren't old either."

Children see themselves as the center of the universe. When problems come up, they often think it's because of something they did. It's important to separate grownup problems from children's problems. A child whose parents are divorcing may need to be told over and over, "Mommy left because she and I weren't happy living together anymore. It's not your fault at all. Mommy loves you and I love you and we both think you're a wonderful kid."

Anger is also a normal part of grief. When two-year-old Mara's father came home after being in the hospital, he could hardly wait to see his daughter. But Mara turned her face away. Then, with a sweep of her arm, she threw a bunch of toys off the shelf. Even though he was hurt by Mara's anger, Mara's father said, "It looks like you're pretty mad that I got sick.

That's okay. Everybody feels that way sometimes. I love you and I'm glad to see you, even if you're angry."

Reading books together can help children talk about their experiences and feel that they are not the only ones having these things happen. There are some excellent children's books about children facing different kinds of loss. A few suggestions are listed in the Resource Section.

Grief from loss is a part of life. By helping our toddlers to face the feelings that come with grief, we are teaching them how to cope with the world as it really is.

Questions to ask when a young child faces change are:

- What loss for my child results from this change?

- What feelings might my child have because of this loss?

- What feelings do I have because of this loss?

- What behavior is my child showing as an outlet for these feelings?

- What do I want my child to learn from the way I handle this situation?

24

Ask For Help
When You Need It

CHILDREN ADD STRESS to our lives as well as joy. Sometimes the stress takes over and we lose control, especially if we don't share the load with another adult. When this happens, we can be dangerous to our children. We need to know what to do when we feel ourselves beginning to explode.

"Please go to Johnny," said Johnny's father to his wife. "It's the sixth time he's woken up tonight, and if I go in there I'm afraid I'll throw him on the floor."

"Take Lindsey for awhile," Lindsey's mother begged her neighbor. "I'm so upset about losing my job. If she whines at me one more time, I don't know what I'll do!"

Sometimes we have to get our children away from us for their own protection. "I was so mad at

Jasper," remembered his mother. "My boyfriend was coming for dinner. I had just cleaned up everything, and Jasper dumped his milk on the floor. I grabbed him, ready to shove his face in the milk. Then I remembered how my father used to do that to me, and how scary it was. I put Jasper in his bed and screamed at him to stay there until I could calm down."

It's okay to get mad at our kids. It's not okay to allow ourselves or anyone else to scare or hurt them. If we can't stop this from happening, we must ask someone for help. This could be a friend, a relative, a counselor, a minister, or anyone willing to listen without judging. If you don't know who to ask, go online and search for a parental stress hotline or parent support center.

It's amazing how much just talking to someone and blowing off steam can help. "I felt such hate for Jasper at that moment that it scared me," said his mother, continuing her story. "I just had to talk with someone, but who? We were new in town. I had no friends, and I didn't get along well with my folks. I found the telephone number of a hotline for parents on a paper I'd picked up in the laundromat, and dialed the number. When it rang, I almost hung up, embarrassed at the idea of talking to a stranger. But the lady who answered was so nice and sounded like she cared so much that I found myself telling her about everything. Not just Jasper, but how lonely I was. And how much I wanted my new boyfriend to like me. I hung up feeling better, knowing I could call any time."

"When I got back to the kitchen, Jasper was under the table, trying to clean up the milk. He'd spread it all over the floor, and all over himself. Laughing and crying, I picked him up and hugged him, knowing how much I loved him and how empty my life would be without him."

25

Stop Feeling Guilty

WE ALL KNOW the feelings.

When the child care center teacher told Paul that his son had spent most of the day trying to bite the other children, Paul blamed himself. "Maybe it was because I got mad at him before we came this morning . . . Or maybe I'm not spending enough time with him . . . Or maybe I'm not getting him to eat enough vegetables . . . Or maybe . . . "

"I think maybe," the teacher interrupted gently, "he started out by pretending to be a dog, and then got carried away."

When Jennifer's one-year-old daughter tried climbing onto the kitchen chair, Jennifer rushed to stop her, but wasn't in time. Her daughter toppled over and cut her forehead on the edge of the counter badly enough to need stitches. At the hospital, Jennifer wept, "I let my baby get hurt. I should have watched her more closely. How could I have let this happen?"

The emergency room nurse smiled. "I've got four kids. I must have been in here a dozen times," she said. "The only way you could watch your little girl closely enough to keep something like this from ever happening would be if you spent every minute of your day holding on to her. That would be bad for both of you, much worse than a few stitches."

As parents, we feel strongly about what our children do and what happens to them. When something goes wrong, we almost always feel guilty. We tell ourselves over and over what we did wrong. But we are only a part of our children's lives. They need the freedom to have their own thoughts, feelings, and actions. And they live in a world over which we don't have total control.

Sometimes we do make mistakes. So does everybody. Instead of feeling guilty, we want to learn from our mistakes so we'll do a better job next time. We certainly want our children to learn that way. As a school teacher and mother of two put it, "I'd hate for my kids to get the idea that they must feel rotten every time they make a mistake. That way they'd never try to do anything."

Guilt is normal, but it doesn't help us be better parents. It just spoils our fun. Guilt keeps us looking backward and feeling bad about what we should have done instead of looking forward and feeling good about what we're going to do next.

"DENNIS THE MENACE®" used by permission of Hank Ketcham and © by News America Syndicate.

26

Enjoy Your Child

*C*HILDHOOD PASSES QUICKLY. And it never comes back. As one father, the head of a big company, said. "I could easily spend all my time working. We'd get ahead much faster if I did. But for what? My children will only be small once. The work will still be there to do in a few years when they're older. They won't need me as much then as they do right now."

Sometimes our fun gets spoiled by all the "ought to's" in our lives. It's a beautiful day, just right for a picnic, but we "ought to" get the weeds pulled in our yard, so we don't go. Or we think we can't go on a picnic because there "ought to" be special food, and we only have peanut butter sandwiches. Or we go, but fight with our kids because they "ought to" keep their clothes cleaner.

A mother of five young children, about to be operated on for cancer, said, "I've wasted so much of my time with my kids being upset about such silly things. Or getting caught up in dumb T.V. programs instead of listening to them. If I get through this okay, I'm going to make the most of everything that happens from now on. Sure, I'll get mad sometimes, but not as much and not as often. I'll just be so glad that we can be together."

The good times we have with our kids now will be with us for the rest of our lives. A father whose children are now adults said, "My kids and I have our ups and downs like all people do, but we have so many happy memories. How can we help but be good friends now?"

Part Three

*Finding and Keeping
Quality Child Care*

CHOOSING CHILD CARE is an important decision. It might be a friend we trade child care with for a few hours. It might be a day care home. It might be a large center. Whichever we choose, letting someone else take care of our children means trusting them with the most precious thing in our lives. It's worth taking the time to look at all of the choices and to check them out carefully.

When to Look

"With my first child, I waited to look until I really needed the care. The program I wanted had a waiting list a year long. With the second child, I put my name on the list as soon as I found out I was pregnant."

Where to Look

1. Ask friends who have children in child care where and how they arranged this care. Ask friends if they are interested in trading or in sharing the cost of a person to do care for both families.

2. Call your friends to find out if they know someone looking for child care employment. Ask them to ask the people they hire for child care if they have friends who might be interested.

3. Make an announcement that you're looking for care at a class for parents.

4. Look in the yellow pages of the telephone book under "Child Care."

5. Ask for a list of centers and family day care homes from your county or city offices or from a family resource program.

6. Look on-line for lists of local providers.

7. Look on the bulletin boards at the places where parents with children go - schools, laundromats, bookstores, clothing stores, parks. Leave your own notice.

8. Put a notice with the employment office of a college or university. Post at the Early Childhood Education and Psychology departments as well as general job boards.

9. Look for the telephone number of a local or

regional early childhood education resource center.

10. Call child care centers and see if they're willing to share their substitute lists.

How to Look

1. Figure out what you're able and willing to pay. To get an idea of what's fair, ask friends what they pay per hour and find out what child care centers pay their workers. When you pay someone to do care in your home, remember that you may need to pay federal and state payroll taxes. Call the Internal Revenue Service toll free number for more information.

2. Make a telephone call to possible places or people and ask questions. Questions that can help decide whether a place fits a family's personal situation include:

   • Are you available the days and hours we need?

   • What holidays are you closed or unavailable?

   • What do you charge?

   • Do I have to pay if my child is sick or on vacation?

   • What are your back up plans if you are sick?

   • How close are you to where I live, work, or go to school?

   • Are diapers and meals provided?

Questions that help screen for quality of care include:

- How many children do you care for at
- one time?

- What are their ages?

- For each adult, how many children are there?

- How long have you been doing this? Do you enjoy it? Why?

- What kinds of activities (e.g. water play, sandbox, swings) do you offer? Does a child have the freedom to choose between activities?

- What is your philosophy about toilet training?

- What is your philosophy about discipline?

3. Pick out the places to visit or people to interview which seem to come closest to meeting your personal needs and quality standards. Decide what trade-offs you're willing to make based on what is most important for you and your child. For example, a lower cost home situation which is more personal versus a higher cost center situation which has more structured activities to offer your child. Make an appointment when you can meet without your child.

4. Pay attention to your first impression.

- Do the children look like their needs are being met?

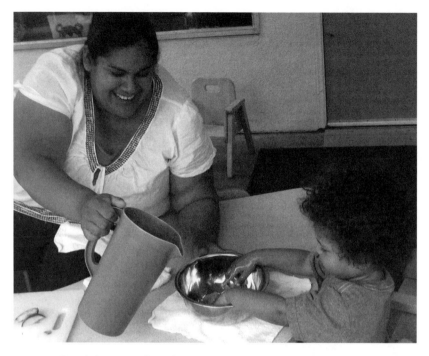

- Is this a safe, clean, and happy place?

- Is this a capable, loving person?

5. When visiting a home or center, watch for awhile and ask yourself or find out:

- How do the caregivers act with the children?

  » Are they caring and friendly?

  » Do they kneel down or otherwise bring themselves close to the children?

  » Do they hug children or hold them on laps?

  » Do they talk more with each other or with the children?

- Are play areas well organized?

  » Are there interesting toys and equipment?

  » Are there lots of different things for the children to do?

  » Are things the right size for the ages of the children? No tiny toys for toddlers to swallow or high slides for them to fall from?

  » Are there enough materials to go around?

  » Is there enough room for the number of children?

  » Are there definite inside and outside play areas?

- Are all the indoor and outdoor areas safe?
  - » Are there any sharp edges?
  - » Are wall plugs covered?
  - » Are medicines and detergents out of reach?
  - » Are fire exits present?
  - » Is the fire extinguisher in working order?
  - » Are things clean?
  - » Are children protected from furnaces, stairs, traffic, etc.?
  - » Where are meals eaten? Naps taken?
  - » What is the changing area and bathroom like?
- How does the staff-to-child ratio compare to other places?
  - » Is someone watching the children at all times?
  - » Do they respond quickly when needed?
  - » How are problems handled?
  - » What kinds of discipline are used?
- How do parents find out what each child's day was like?
  - » Is there someone to talk with?
  - » Are records kept?

- What kinds of activities are done with the children?

  » Are children forced to participate or can they pick and choose?

  » Do caregivers do things for the children or do they help them to do things for themselves?

  » Is there a television? A computer? How much time is it on?

- What are mealtimes like?

  » Is healthy, simple food served?

  » Are meals served often enough?

- How are diapering and toilet training handled?

  » Is toilet training pushed or relaxed?

- How are emergencies handled?

  » Are emergency cards kept on each child?

  » Are there plans in case of disaster?

  » Are any of the caregivers trained in first aid?

- Who will take care of the children if the caregiver is sick?

- Do children have a comfortable place to nap?

  » Are they helped with naps in a loving way?

  » Do they nap when they're tired or is there a scheduled nap time?

- Is there a sickness policy?
  - » Who decides if a child is sick?
- Do the children seem happy and comfortable?
  - » Are they playing or talking freely with each other and the caregivers?

6. Both in centers and with caregivers in your own home, interview the person who will be taking care of your child. Ask questions to get the person talking, like:

- How long have you been doing this?

- Do you have special training or experience? For example, first aid?

- Why do you do this kind of work?

- What do you feel you have to offer the children?

- (If the care is in your own home): What are you willing to do in the way of cleaning up?

- What would you do if a child tried to hit you or another child?

- What would you do if a child was sitting alone looking upset?

- What would you do if . . . (pick the thing your child does that worries you the most)?

If you act interested and friendly, people are usually flattered and pleased to answer your questions. After all, you're showing that you think what they do is important. No matter how good a reputation a center might have, the kind of care your child will have depends on the kind of person who is actually caring for your child. Do you feel comfortable with this person?

7. Ask for names and telephone numbers of people who've had their children cared for by the individual or center you're considering. For centers, ask questions like:

   - When did your child go to the center? For how long?

- How old was your child at the time?

- Was your child happy at the center? What was done worst . . . and best?

- If you could choose again, would you choose the same center? Why?

For individual caregivers, ask questions like:

- When did you hire this person? For how long?

- How old was your child at the time?

- What do you feel the person did best?

- What was done worst?

- Did this person get to work on time?

- Would you hire this person again? Why?

8. Pick the places or people you like the best and set up a second visit (at a different time of day) or interview. Have your child with you this time. Ask yourself:

   - What do people do to help my child feel welcome and comfortable with them?

   - Is respect shown for my child's shyness with strangers, or do people seem annoyed?

   - Does my child seem interested in the activities, toys, and equipment?

   - How does my child react to this place/or caregiver?

9. Make your decision. Ask yourself:

- Will this person/program meet my needs?

- Will this person/program meet my child's needs?

- What will my child learn from being with this program/person?

- Do I feel comfortable leaving my child with this person or at this center?

Keep Track of What's Going On

1. Every day when you pick up your child, ask the person who is with your child:

   • What did my child do today?

   • Were there any problems?

   • When did my toddler, eat, sleep, have a diaper change/use the toilet?

2. If your child has been hurt in any way, find out exactly what happened:

   • How did he happen to fall?

   • Where did that bruise on her arm come from?

   • What first aid was done?

3. If your child seems unhappy, ask yourself:

   • Is she crying because she's afraid of the people or place, or is she unhappy that I'm going away?

   • Does my child stay unhappy after I'm gone? (It might be possible to wait and listen outside the door where your child can't see you, or ask a friend who's bringing a child later to see how your child is doing.)

4. If your child stays unhappy over a period of time, talk with the caregiver. For some children, it takes longer to adjust. You may need to be patient. One mother found that her little boy didn't know what to do with himself for the last hour of the day. She

arranged to have him picked up a little earlier, and suddenly he was fine.

5. If this doesn't help, go back and observe. Each child is different, and the right place for one child might be wrong for another. One father saw that all the children were older than his daughter and played together in a group. His daughter just sat alone by herself a lot of the time. He put her in a small day care home with a couple of children her own age, and she was much happier.

6. Listen when the caregiver tries to tell you something about your child. This person sees your child doing things you don't. It's hard not to feel attacked when someone tells us that our children are being particularly testy (i.e., spitting, hitting, pushing) but we may learn something by listening.

7. Be honest with the caregiver about things you think need improvement. Be positive. A statement like: "Next time, I'd like you to make sure Elli wears her jacket when she goes outside" works better than "How could you let Elli go outside with no jacket!"

8. Let the people who take care of your children know how much you appreciate them. It's hard work for not enough money. Take the time to say "thank you" every chance you get. Statements like: "She had such a happy day with you last time and

couldn't wait to get here" or "I like the way you let me know about Jason's biting, and your suggestions really helped" can let a care-giver end a long day feeling like it's all worth doing.

9. Be aware of changes that might affect the quality of care your child is receiving. Pay attention to the consistency of care. Staff changes in a center may mean that a different person is with your child. How do you feel about this individual? In an in-home situation, notice any changes that might affect how well your caregiver is able to do his or her job. For example, additional children, added stress in personal life, etc.

Have a Plan for When Your Child is Sick

Children who are really sick do not belong in group situations. A child with fever, an upset stomach, diarrhea, a bad cold, or who's not feeling well, needs to be with a parent or friend.

Keeping children home when they are sick is important to our children as well as to the others being cared for. Besides spreading the illness, a sick child has a lower resistance. Being with other children is stressful, and a child can take much longer to get well. Or even catch another bug. And a sick child needs special comforting.

Young children often do get sick, especially when they first start spending time in a group situation. It makes sense to figure out ahead of time how care for a sick child will be handled. Possibilities are:

- Arrange with an employer to take work home when a child is sick. It's important to be realistic about whether any work will really get done with a sick child.

- Make a list of friends to call.

- Find someone to do child care who's willing to take care of sick children.

- Find out whether your community has a sick child care program. Visit this program to see whether it might meet your child's needs.

- Share this responsibility equally with both parents. The deciding question can be, "Which of us can miss work most easily today?" or "Whose turn is it?"

Whether it's for a few hours while we take time for ourselves, or all day, five days a week while we work at a full-time job, the people and places where we leave our children are important. The ways in which they are cared for will shape our toddlers' view of what the world outside their homes and people other than family members are like. The time spent in the best kind of care will help them to grow in understanding and self-confidence.

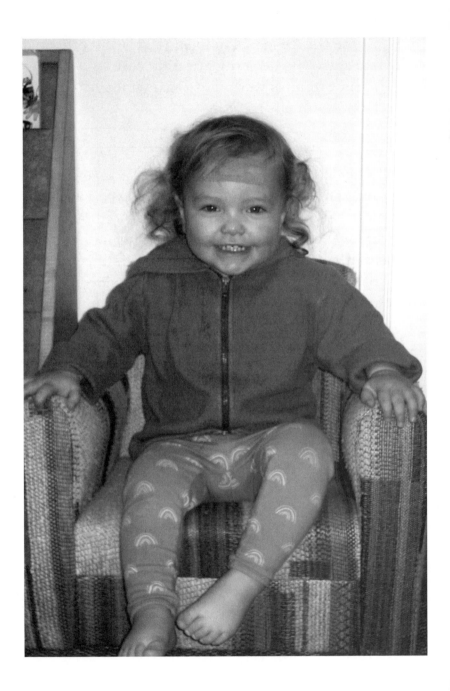

27

Conclusion

THE TODDLER AGE is a wonderful and exciting time in a child's life. To a toddler, the world is new and here to be explored; everything seems possible and amazing.

As we live and play with our toddlers, we see glimpses of the adults they'll grow up to be some day. We have a tremendous opportunity to build on their curiosity and to encourage their drive to learn, giving them an approach to life that will stay with them always.

This is a time when our children are the closest to us in their thoughts and feelings. As they get older, they'll be more interested in the outside world and in other kids. But for toddlers, parents are the most important people in their lives.

The respect we show our toddlers and ourselves now will help them build respect for themselves and for us. The closeness and understanding we gain lays a strong foundation for the relationship we will have with our children for the rest of our lives.

Appendix 1
Resource List

THIS RESOURCE LIST will hopefully offer some useful suggestions about where you can find further information on parenting and the toddler years. It is by no means a complete list, but is meant to provide some direction for those wanting to read more.

Happy Reading

Baby Hearts: A Guide to Giving Your Child an Emotional Head Start, by Susan Goodwyn Ph.D. and Linda Acredolo Ph.D. (Bantam Dell, New York, 2005). Research-based advice and activities to foster your child's emotional skills between birth and age 3.

Becoming the Parent You Want To Be, by Laura Davis and Janis Keyser. (Broadway Books, New York, 1997). Provides straightforward approaches to everyday questions and struggles faced by parents of young children, birth to five. Highly recommended.

<u>Dear Parent: Caring for Infants with Respect</u>, by
Magda Gerber, edited by Joan Weaver (RIE, Los
Angeles, 2003)
A collection of essays and talks by Magda Gerber,
founder of the RIE institute.

Helping Your Child Sleep Through the Night, by
Joanne Cuthbertson and Susie Schevill
(Doubleday & Co., Inc., New York, 1985).
A step-by-step guide for how to deal with sleep
problems. It offers good, clear suggestions for what
to do for your child and yourself when your child
is having trouble sleeping.

Infants, Toddlers, and Caregivers, by Janet Gonzalez-
Mena and Dianne Widmeyer Eyer. (McGraw-Hill,
New York, 2008).
Lots of examples to help us see the world from
the very young child's point of view. Tells how to
provide care in a loving, respectful way that will
help children to grow.

It's My Body, by L. Freeman. (Parenting Press,
Washington, 1984).
Helps give children an awareness of their rights
to protect their own bodies from uncomfortable touch.

Kidpower Teenpower Fullpower International,
Provides personal safety advice, articles and training.
Teaches how to prevent child abuse, bullying and
other personal safety problems. www.kidpower.org.

Liberated Parents, Liberated Children: Your Guide
To A Happier Family, by Adele Faber & Elaine
Mazlish. (Avon Books, New York, 1990).
An excellent book on how to apply reflective

listening skills in your day-to-day life with children of all ages.

The Magic Years, by Selma H. Fraiberg. (Charles Scribner's Sons, New York, 1996).
Gives a perspective on understanding and handling the problems of early childhood. This is a child development classic, written from a psychoanalytic point of view.

Parents' Book of Toilet Teaching, by Joanna Cole. (Ballantine Books, New York, 1999).
A discussion of toilet learning considered from the starting point of the child's needs.

P.E.T. (Parent Effectiveness Training), by Thomas Gordan. (Three Rivers Press, New York, 2000).
Effective techniques to help parents related to their children in ways that enhance self-esteem.

Protect the Gift: Keeping Children and Teens Safe, by Gavin deBecker. (Dell, New York, 2000).
Practical advice for parents of children and teens by a renowned safety expert.

Raising Your Spirited Child, by Mary Sheedy Kurcinka. (Harper-Collins Publishers, New York, 2006).
A very accessible book with specific strategies that work for all children, as well as "spirited" children. Highly recommended.

The RIE Institute (Resources for Infant Educarers)
was founded in 1978 as a non-profit membership
organization concerned with improving the
care and education of infants. The institute
offers parent-infant guidance classes, trainings,
workshops and conferences for professionals. For
more information go to www.rie.org.

The Second Twelve Months of Life, by Frank and
Teresa Caplan. (Bantam Books, New York, 1982).
Gives a month-by-month account of the
developmental stages of the second year. Full
of information, and provides a good overview of
development.

<u>Sigh of Relief</u>, by Martin I. Green. (Bantam Books, New York, 1994).
One of the most useful and comprehensive books for childhood emergencies and accident prevention, in an extremely accessible format.

<u>Solve Your Child's Sleep Problems</u>, by Richard Ferber, M.D. (Fireside, New York, 2006).
A matter-of-fact guide for dealing with sleep issues.

<u>Sugar-Free Toddlers</u>, by Susan Watson. (Williamson Publishing, Charlotte, Vermont, 1991).
Lots of healthy, practical recipes that appeal to toddlers.

Things To Do With Toddlers and Twos, by Karen
Miller. (Telshare Publishing Co., Inc., Chelsea,
Massachusetts, 2000).
Gives lots of useful examples of activities young
children will enjoy and learn from. It is aimed
at preschool teachers, but good for parents too.
Also offers good insights into problems, especially
biting.

Toilet Learning, by Alison Mack. (Little Brown,
Boston, 1983).
How to help your child learn to use the toilet
when ready. It has a special section to read to
children.

Toilet Training, by Vicky Lansky. (Book Peddlers,
Minnetonka, Minnesota, 2002).
Practical suggestions for helping toilet learning
happen at the child's pace.

Welcoming Your Second Baby, by Vicky Lansky. (Book
Peddlers, Minnetonka, Minnesota, 2005).
How to prepare your child for the birth of a sibling.
How to handle rivalry and jealously.

Without Spanking Or Spoiling, by Elizabeth Crary.
(Parenting Press, Washington, 1993).
A practical approach to toddler and preschool
guidance. Talks about discipline in a positive light.

Working and Caring, by T. Berry Brazleton.
   (Cambridge, Massachusetts, 1992).
   An examination of some of the decisions and
   dilemmas facing working parents of young children.

The Working Parents' Survival Guide, by Sally
Wendkos Olds. (iUniverse, Lincoln, Nebraska, 2000).
A comprehensive source of information and
support for working parents.

Your Baby and Child From Birth to Age Five, by
Penelope Leach. (Alfred A. Knopf, New York, 1997).
A useful book for parents of young children.
Presents common sense information and expects
parents to decide what is appropriate for them.

Your Child At Play: Two to Three Years, by Marilyn Segal
and Don Adcock. (Newmarket Press, New York, 1999).
Focuses on growing up, language, and the
imagination. Helps parents understand their child's
development during the second and third year of life.

Your Child's Self-Esteem, by Dorothy Corkille Briggs.
(Broadway Books, New York, 2001).
Helps parents to understand how to help children
feel good about themselves.

Your Self-Confident Baby: How to Encourage Your
Child's Natural Abilities—from the very start, by
Magda Gerber and Allison Johnson (John Wiley
and Sons, Inc., New York, 1998)
Easy to read, with lots of examples of applying the
RIE philosophy in parenting infants and toddlers.

Appendix 2

Recipes

The Toddler Center serves organic, whole grain, sugar-free, vegetarian meals and snacks that are both toddler friendly and extraordinarily healthy. Here are a few of the Toddler Center kids' favorites that are sure to please the whole family:

Chilaquiles Toddler Style

What You Need:
8 ounces corn tortillas (up to 10)
3 eggs
Oil for Cooking

How to Make It:
Cut tortillas in half, a few at a time. Then cut into ¼ inch strips. Crack eggs into a mixing bowl and whisk with a fork. Add the tortilla strips and mix to coat. Heat a frying pan on medium high, coated with oil. Add the mixture and cook, stirring occasionally until eggs are completely set. Serve warm. Also great topped with diced tomatoes and avocado.

Hummus

Hummus is packed with protein and iron. Add a simple chopped salad and whole wheat pita and you have a complete meal. This "toddlerized" version has the spice and acidity toned down from many store-bought versions. This recipe makes a lot and can be cut into thirds for a meal for a family—or make the whole amount and store it in the fridge for snacks with whole grain crackers or vegetable strips. It's easy to make, and children love it.

What You Need:
3 15oz cans chickpeas
1/4 cup sesame tahini (sesame butter)
Juice of 1/2 lemon
1/2 clove garlic
1/4 cup virgin olive oil
1/4 teaspoon salt

How to Make It:
Drain garbanzos and rinse in a strainer. Place in food processor (with tahini, lemon juice, garlic, oil and salt. Blend, stop, scrape down the sides of the processer bowl and blend again until smooth. If the hummus is too thick, you can add a little water and blend to the thickness you like.

Beets and Cabbage

People are often surprised to see our toddlers wolfing down vegetables. This dish is a very simple and popular one. The slow roasting brings out the natural sugars in the vegetables. If possible, purchase beets with the greens still attached; they are fresher, tastier and have more vitamins intact.

What You Need:
1 medium head of cabbage
3 large beets
1 apple (optional)
2-3 Tablespoon virgin olive oil
1/4 teaspoon salt

How to Make It:
Preheat oven to 425 degrees. Clean all vegetables well. Cut the cabbage in half and core it. Chop each half in fourths, shred as finely as possible with a knife or with the shredder attachment of a food processor. Peel beets and grate with a hand grater or grater attachment of a food processor. (Grate apple if using.) Combine everything with oil and salt in a 10 x 16 baking pan and toss to coat well. Roast for about 45 minutes to an hour, stirring and turning (with tongs or a spoon) until soft and reduced to about half its volume. Serve warm or cold.

Smoothie Bread

This is a very tasty banana bread that uses only whole fruit to sweeten it. Standard recipes often add up to a whole cup of sugar, but the children love this bread without any added sweeteners. Enjoy with some cottage cheese or yogurt to make a complete snack. The recipe is also dairy and egg free so children with sensitivities can enjoy it.

What You Need:
1 ½ cup whole wheat pastry flour
2 cups rolled oats
2 teaspoons baking powder
1 teaspoon baking soda
4 small bananas (or 3 medium or 2 extra large)
1 pear (or 1 apple)
½ cup unsweetened rice milk
½ cup oil (canola or olive or a mixture)
1 shake salt
1 shake cinnamon
1/3 cup raisins

How to Make It:
Preheat oven to 350 degrees and grease 9 x 12 pan with oil. In a mixing bowl combine all dry ingredients and whisk. Set aside. Combine remaining ingredients in a food processor or blender. Puree until smooth. Combine wet with dry in the bowl until just mixed,

then add raisins. Scrape into greased pan and bake about 40 minutes until golden and completely set in the middle. Allow to cool before slicing.

Soba Salad

Edamame, or green soy beans, are packed with protein, fiber and iron, as are soba noodles, or Japanese buckwheat noodles. Most soba noodles and edamame cook in just 5 minutes, so this eliminates the need for two pots.

What you need:
16 ounce package soba noodles
1 pound frozen, shelled edamame
1 1/2 Tablespoons soy sauce
1 Tablespoon toasted sesame oil
Any vegetables you want. (Some ideas: cooked
    broccoli, cauliflower or bok choy, shredded carrots
    or cabbage, diced cucumber or avocado)
Sesame Seeds

How to make it:
Break noodles into 2 inch long pieces.
Bring about 6 quarts of water to a rolling boil. Add a few shakes of salt, the noodles and the frozen edamame at the same time. Cook for 5 minutes. Test a noodle and a bean for doneness. Drain and rinse with cold water. Toss with soy sauce and sesame oil.

Add any veggies that you want and/or cooked eggs.
Sprinkle with sesame seeds. Serve warm or cold.

Quinoa Fritters with Greens

Quinoa is a mild tasting seed from the Andes,
renowned for being a complete protein. These fritters
are a great way to feed greens to toddlers (and
adults!). The fritters are easy and fun for toddlers to
pick up and eat.

What you need:
1 cup quinoa
1 ¾ cup water
4 ounces fresh basil (leaves only)
4 ounces fresh spinach (or arugula or de-stemmed
Swiss chard or kale or a mixture!)
5 eggs
4 ounces grated cheese (or alternatively, almond meal
and 1 teaspoon soy sauce)
Oil for cooking

How to make it:
Put quinoa in a fine mesh strainer. Thoroughly
wash quinoa under cold running water. Do not skip
washing. (Quinoa has a naturally occurring chemical
layer to protect its seeds from animal predators. If you
do not wash it will taste bitter!)

Place quinoa with water in a pot with a fitted lid and

put on high heat. Bring to a boil, then simmer for 7 minutes. Turn off heat and allow to steam for about 20 minutes. Uncover and allow to cool.

While the quinoa cooks and cools, finely mince the basil and greens. Crack the eggs into a mixing bowl and whisk. Add the greens, cheese and slightly cooled quinoa. Mix.

Heat a griddle or large fry pan on medium high and coat with oil. Drop scoops of about three tablespoons of the quinoa mixture into the hot oil. Flatten into patties, if neccesary. Cook the fritters until golden on one side, then flip with a spatula and allow to brown on the other side. Repeat until you have used up all the batter. Serve warm. Adults enjoy these with dips and salsas.

Here are some special recipes from the Toddler Center, but please note, they are definitely NOT for eating.

Cooked Playdough

This is a favorite project at the Toddler Center. We like to make it using an electric non stick wok/skillet at the table. The children love to help make it (even very young children can pour the measured flour, water or oil into the bowl or wok) as much as they love playing with it.

What you need:
2 cups all purpose flour
1 cup salt
2 tablespoons cream of tartar
2 cups water mixed with desired food coloring
1/4 cup oil

What to do:

Mix all the dry ingredients together in a big pot (a nonstick pot or a cast iron dutch oven works well, but you can use any kind of pot). Add the wet ingredients. Cook and stir and cook and stir and cook and stir until the playdough is dry to the touch. To keep it fresh after it cools, wrap the playdough in plastic or an airtight container.

Bubbles

1/2 cup Dawn liquid dish washing detergent
Add enough water to make 2 quarts
1 1/2 teaspoon glycerine

This formula seems to get better with age. Let it sit around in an open container for at least a day.

Ooblick

This is a wonderful substance for multi-sensory play. It's unique in that it's both liquid and solid-like at the same time. It also cleans up extraordinarily easily.

What you need:
1 box of cornstarch (1 pound)
2 2/3 cups cold water
3 drops of food coloring (optional)

What to do:
Put the cold water and food coloring in a mixing bowl. Add the cornstarch a little at a time while stirring until the ooblick is at a desired consistency.

About Jen the Cook

Jen Vered has a BA degree in Environmental Studies from UCSC, where she studied sustainable agriculture and food systems. Jen began cooking professionally in a restaurant in Tel Aviv and returned to the U.S. to go to culinary school in the Napa Valley.

In 2004, Jen came to work at the Toddler Center and started her own catering business. She lives in Ben Lomond with her son Amir, her husband, Shai, and their three cats. Jen dreams of a world where everyone can eat organic, sustainable food, like the children at the Toddler Center.

Appendix 3

*Safety Tips for
Parents of Toddlers*

Put safety first. Don't let inconvenience, fear of offending someone, or embarrasement stop you from staying in charge of the emotional and physical safety of your child.

There is no substitute for constant supervision. Young children do not always have the understanding or the skills to recognize potential danger – whether from an animal, a cliff, a piece of glass, an electric outlet, a car or a person who might be unsafe.

These tips are based on the article titled "People Safety for Toddlers" from Kidpower's program. For more information, see 'About the Author' or visit www.kidpower.org.

Pay attention to your own intuition. If you are even a little bit uncomfortable about a person or a situation involving your child, take action rather than hope that the problem will go away by itself. No matter what the relationship, your job is to speak up, stick around, intervene and keep watching until your concerns are addressed.

Set a good example. Model respectful behavior by using your words, advocating for yourself, waiting your turn and being careful.

Give kids practice in taking charge. While playing tickling or roughhousing games, teach children that their "No" means "No" and their "Stop" means "Stop". For example, when playing a chasing game such as "I'm going to get you!" – sometimes have the children stop you by turning, putting their hand out in front of them and yelling "STOP!" Your immediate response provides an important lesson in personal power.

Accept children's right to be upset or have unhappy feelings when setting appropriate limits. For example, during a car seat struggle, say calmly, "I see you are mad. You don't want to get in your car seat. It's not a choice. The car seat keeps you safe."

Empower children with choices when you can. Allowing children to choose between the red cup or the blue cup, walking by themselves or being carried, or doing something right away or in five minutes, helps children develop decision-making skills and gives them a sense of power.

Remember that affection should always be a child's choice. Let children choose hugging or kissing, even with Grandma. Teach children how to move away from unwanted touch or teasing and say, "Stop. I don't like that." Tell adults or other children to respect the child's wishes by listening and stopping.

Listen to Children. Even if their fears seem insignificant to you, listen with compassion.

About the Author

When *1,2,3...The Toddler Years* was first written, author Irene van der Zande was the mother of two young children and a consultant to nonprofits on organization development and management. Irene had gained a reputation for helping people and organizations to define and structure their goals and ideas into successful projects and programs.

In 1984, Irene was approached by Toddler Center Co-Directors Vickey and Lise who asked Irene to help them figure out how to turn their dream of creating a book reflecting their philosophy into a reality. She ended up writing it. Through hundreds of hours of discussions with Toddler Center staff, Irene was able to capture the essence of the Toddler Center approach in a fashion useful and interesting to parents. Toddler Center staff involvement ensured that the ideas and their examples offered an accurate reflection of their program. Irene also provided extensive consultation on funding and marketing strategies for the book.

Most of all, though, it was Irene's experiences as the mother of young children that made this kind of book possible. As her daughter Chantal at age 8 put it:

"Me and my little brother taught
her everything she knows!"

Irene with her family in 1985

In 1985, the year that ***1,2,3...The Toddler Years*** was first written, Irene protected a group of young children, including her own daughter and son, from a man who was threatening to kidnap them. This experience inspired Irene to join with experts and parents to start Kidpower - an international nonprofit leader that is dedicated to empowering and protecting people of all ages and abilities.

Since being established in 1989, Kidpower has served over a million children, teens, and adults, including those with special needs, of many different cultures locally and around the world. As Kidpower's co-founder, executive director, and primary author, Irene has led the creation of programs, writing of curriculum, training of instructors, and development of centers.

Kidpower shares the Toddler Center's values of creating a community of respect, safety, caring, and confidence for children and their grown-ups.

Irene's publications include *Bullying - What Adults Need to Know and Do to Keep Kids Safe*, the *Kidpower Guide for Parents and Teachers*, the *Kidpower Safety Plan Comic Book*, the *Relationship Safety Handbook*, and numerous training manuals and articles. Visit **www.kidpower.org** for information about the wealth of free resources in the on-line library, publications for sale, and workshops.

Today, Irene is the grandmother of a toddler and is enjoying once again being an important part of the life of a young child.

Index

BOOK ORDER FORM

Santa Cruz
TODDLER CARE CENTER
1738 16th Avenue
Santa Cruz, CA 95062
Respect for Children

Phone: (831) 476-4120
Fax: (831) 476-4277
www.sctcc.org

Please send me _____ copies of
1,2,3...The Toddler Years @ $14.95 each $ _____
    ($16.37 for California residents)
    Shipping:
    $3.00 for the first book,
    $2.00 for each additional book $ _____
                 Total Enclosed $ _____

Charge my VISA/MC:

#_____ Exp. Date _____

Check or money order enclosed payable to: **SCTCC**
No cash or COD's. Please allow 3-4 weeks for shipment.

Name:_____

Address:_____

City/State:_____ Zip:_____

BOOK ORDER FORM

Santa Cruz
TODDLER CARE CENTER
1738 16th Avenue
Santa Cruz, CA 95062
Respect for Children

Phone: (831) 476-4120
Fax: (831) 476-4277
www.sctcc.org

Please send me _____ copies of
1,2,3...The Toddler Years @ $14.95 each $ _____
    ($16.37 for California residents)
    Shipping:
    $3.00 for the first book,
    $2.00 for each additional book $ _____
                 Total Enclosed $ _____

Charge my VISA/MC:

#_____ Exp. Date _____

Check or money order enclosed payable to: **SCTCC**
No cash or COD's. Please allow 3-4 weeks for shipment.

Name:_____

Address:_____

City/State:_____ Zip:_____

The Santa Cruz Toddler Care Center is a private non-profit organization. Because the Toddler Center is committed to making its services available on the basis of need, the tuition each family pays does not cover the cost of the child's care.

You can help. Your tax-deductible contribution will express your commitment and support for quality childcare.

Thanks for your help.

HERE'S MY CONTRIBUTION

O $200   O $100   O $50   O $25   O $15   O $ _____

Please charge my VISA/MC # _____

Exp. Date _____

Name _____

Address _____

City _____ Zip _____

Santa Cruz
TODDLER CARE CENTER
1738 16th Avenue
Santa Cruz, CA 95062
Respect for Children

HERE'S MY CONTRIBUTION

O $200   O $100   O $50   O $25   O $15   O $ _____

Please charge my VISA/MC # _____

Exp. Date _____

Name _____

Address _____

City _____ Zip _____

Santa Cruz
TODDLER CARE CENTER
1738 16th Avenue
Santa Cruz, CA 95062
Respect for Children